There's Nothing Funny About Running

THERE'S NOTHING FUNNY ABOUT RUNNING

BY TIMOTHY L. MARTIN

Marathon Publishers, Inc.
Sacramento, California

THERE'S NOTHING FUNNY ABOUT RUNNING © 1999 by Timothy L. Martin

10 9 8 7 6 5 4 3 2 1

Cover art and drawings © 1999 by Duane Flatmo

Library of Congress Catalog Card Number: 99-74640

ISBN 0-9655187-8-7

Distributed to the book trade by Independent Publishers Group (800.888.4741).

Individuals may order directly from the publisher, Marathon Publishers, Inc. (888.586.9099), but please check your local bookstore first.

Printed in the United States of America

To Linda

My running partner, my editor,
my inspiration, the mother of
our children, and, as luck
would have it, my wife.

Contents

Acknowledgments

I am indebted to the members of Six Rivers Running Club for their limitless help and support. I would also like to express my gratitude to Rich Benyo, editor of *Marathon & Beyond*.

Also, special thanks to Dennis Craythorn and Rich Hanna, of Marathon Publishers, for appreciating the beauty in laughter and running.

Tim Martin
McKinleyville, California

Some Thoughts On Lightening Up

This is where I was supposed to write something uplifting about running, maybe a few pages about how it lowers cholesterol, reduces stress and promotes cardiovascular fitness. I should also include a page or two about how running is quick, simple and inexpensive (you don't need a ski mask and a fast getaway car to afford it). I should tell you how it builds confidence, promotes weight loss, cures tension, and so on. Ideally, by the time I had finished, you couldn't wait to turn the page and gobble up all the useful facts and information contained within.

But, frankly, all that stuff is boring. As dull as an infomercial knife set. If you ask me, and I could have sworn somebody did, the world is overloaded with facts and information. I'm tired of reading about how to Train Like A Champion or Shave 10 Minutes Off My Marathon Time. What I'd like to hear more about is the part of running that seldom gets mentioned: the fun part. I'd like to read about the buzz of adrenaline runners get when they lace up their shoes and the lingering effects of endorphins after a simple jog in the forest. I'd like to read about belligerent race directors, comical road trips and spouses who procrastinate for hours before they run. I want to read about soul-searching runs, outrageous races and inspirational friends. In short, I want to experience, firsthand, the courage, camaraderie and humor of running.

Evidently, I'm not alone. In his book, *Thoughts on the Run*, Joe Henderson writes: "A 'Run for Fun' book is needed because 99% of running literature is written for about only 1% of the runners—those who have the interest, ability and opportunity to win anything bigger than an intramural mile. The information contained is impractical and misleading—if not downright dangerous—for the rest. And 99.9% of the writings are wholly negative in tone—all hurt, fight and sacrifice. They tell what running takes, not what it gives. They scare as many readers as they help."

They probably scare other people, as well. Most of the non-runners I know would rather drink Guiness Stout from John Popper's harmonica than accompany me on a run around the block. They see only the unpleasant side of running. They ask questions like, "Why do you put yourself through all that pain and fatigue?" "What are you, a masochist?" And, "If running is so much fun, why don't I ever see a smiling runner?"

I reply, "Runners *do* smile. You've just been looking in the wrong places."

Take, for instance, that place where you begin your daily run. First, there's the ecstatic pre-run smile as you prepare for your workout and you picture the adventure awaiting you around every bend. Then there's the peaceful mid-run "I think I'm in heaven" smile as the stress bleeds from your pores and you feel a cleansing that even a shaved head and a new pair of Nikes couldn't give you. Finally, there's the satisfied post-run smile. To some, it may not look like a smile at all, but it's there, all right. Just look in the mirror.

The plain truth is, running is not all fatigue, pain and missing toenails. It's also peace, euphoria, exhilaration and accomplishment. But more than anything, it's a fist-pumping blast, if you allow it to be. The fun part of running lies within all of us, we just need to let it out.

So put away your log book. Forget about mile splits. Don't worry about lapsed times or Personal Records. Take a peaceful jog along the beach, or maybe a long, slow run on a muddy path. Squish, squish, squish. There, doesn't that feel better? While you're at it, take off those shoes and wiggle your toes.

And remember, don't ever let anyone tell you there's nothing funny about running.

SOMEBODY STOP ME!

Fantastic tales on the obsession for running

Running Off At The Mouth

My wife is worried about me. She's beginning to wonder if I should see a doctor. The head-peeper kind of doctor. My problem, so I'm told, is an acute obsession with swift forward movement by sheer physical effort. In other words, I'm a running zealot (5:00 a.m. breed).

Personally, I like to think of myself as more of a running devotee, but, according to my wife, I'm nothing less than an addicted runner. Lately she's even begun to regard me with the kind of wary contempt reserved for a stupid dog which may bite. After all, a disease such as this might be contagious. It might take her down the same path of insanity that I'm already traversing.

I can't help the way I feel about running. It's the perfect sport. I prophetize whenever I can get anyone to listen (and even when I can't) that running is the greatest thing since sliced bread—it's even more fun than an old E-ticket at Disneyland. It is, in fact, give us a drum roll, please, maestro—THE ANSWER TO EVERYTHING.

My wife considers running fiercely illogical. According to her, "running for fun" is only the warp and woof of fantasy. Mention running around our house and she cracks ten knuckles, turns up a radio or suddenly remembers something she forgot to do. Even our dog slinks out of the room, an uneasy deserter's grin on its face. That's okay. Throughout history men and women of vision have always had to endure the barbs of ridicule. You learn to live with these things or you end up in a small room writing letters to home with Crayolas.

It was no mean trick getting my wife to give running a try. She was a tough nut to crack. I put in as many miles with my brain as I did with my feet talking to her, cajoling, pleading. Nothing seemed to work.

But patience has its virtue. At least in this case it did. The Big Breakthrough came just the other day and it came as most breakthroughs do, stealthily and on little cat's feet. . . and when I least expected it.

We had just finished breakfast and were sitting at the kitchen table when I said, "It's sure a beautiful day. I can't wait to get out for a run."

Linda pulled a face. "Right. Beating your knees to a frazzle sounds like the perfect way to spend Saturday morning."

"I've been running for years," I said, with an angry sniff, "and there's nothing wrong with my knees."

"Except that they're probably on their last leg," she replied.

"Let's get something straight," I said, trying to light the fires of righteous indignation. "Contrary to what you think, running is great exercise. It strengthens your heart. It keeps you fit and healthy. It even increases longevity. And that's just a small part of what the sport has to offer."

"That may be, but..."

"Wait a minute. Let me finish," I said, eyeing her with all the baleful interrupt-if-you-dare pugnacity of Captain Quigg of the Bounty. "Not only is running beneficial to your health, it's good for your mind. It relieves stress, builds confidence and gives you a fresher outlook on life." The words were gushing out in torrents, all the marvelous things about running. When I had finished, I readied myself for her fiery rebuttal.

Oddly enough, it never came.

Instead, a thinking frown spread over Linda's face. "Maybe you're right," she said.

My mouth dropped open. I struggled for words. "Wha...? Are you serious?"

"I sure am," she said. And then, without any preamble, "I've been thinking about starting up an exercise program. I might even try running."

My face said I didn't believe a word of it.

"I'm serious," she said. "I promise, I will."

"All right, I'm going to take you up on that promise, right on the spot. *Right on the spot.*" I emphasized intensifier, preposition and object by tapping a spoon against my water glass. "Let's go running today!"

"Today?" She stared at me with her lower jaw sprung ajar.

"As soon as you put on some running clothes." A long groan arose in the air and seemed to take possession of the very morning. I smiled. "Come on, look at it as an adventure," I said. "Didn't you ever fly a kite? Go hiking?"

"Escape from Alcatraz?" she said. But any argument was futile now, and she knew it. She had given her word. While my wife shuffled upstairs to change, I plopped down on the couch, grinning from ear to ear. I could hardly wait to get started.

A few minutes later we headed out. Our pace was modest and I fell in behind where I immediately began instructing. "Beginners expend a lot of energy doing everything wrong," I said. "It's going to take awhile before you evolve into a smooth efficient athlete such as my..." Suddenly she sprinted off at breakneck speed, leaving me far behind.

"Hey," I shouted. "Too fast! Too fast!" She didn't listen. Beginners, I thought, chuckling to myself. They run like newspaper burns, fast, hot and quick to die. She'll be exhausted before the end of the block.

Five miles later, as a trickle of sweat wormed its way down the side of my forehead, I was still trying to catch up and losing ground rapidly. My wife was just a dot in the distance.

She ran with a speed that was startling. How could she be so good her first time out? And if she was this good already, how much better would she be with a little training? Fast? Real fast? Super fast? My mind, long past cooperation, refused to even consider it.

"Wake up..."

"Wake up, honey." My wife was standing over me, shaking my shoulder. "I'm ready to go. I'll meet you outside."

I had been dreaming. Not one of my Imperial Rome dreams, courtesy of Hollywood, California, but more of a I-Think-I've-Created-a-Monster dream. Ha! What a hotbed of nonsense my subconscious was to invent such fictions. I pulled on my shoes and started out the door.

A sudden stab of doubt. Suppose she really was that fast? I ran back inside and slipped on a pair of racing flats. Just to be safe, of course.

As it turned out, Linda didn't set any records that day, but she did show a great deal of determination and, best of all, she enjoyed herself. She even wants to continue running with me, as long as I promise not to go too fast.

And that's the kind of promise I can live with.

The Untouchables

We keep hearing what a dangerous world this is. I'm beginning to believe it. We always seem to be poised on the stage of something dreadful: plague, famine, stock-market crash, terrorist attacks, nuclear war, freeway snipers, toxic mouthwash or a merry combination of them all. A pit bull could eat your face.

And if that's not enough, we now have a peril specifically tailored to the running community—a calamity that can cause even the most civilized and erudite members of the family to start nipping at one another. A crisis comparable to Watergate, Iranscam and Chernobyl. It's the shocking tragedy of the vandalized—

T-shirt!

Yes, a T-shirt. But not just any T-shirt. Not Value Pak's six-for-a-buck super saver special, or La Palay's designer brand with diamonds embedded in the cuff. And certainly not the "rock shirt," this year's litmus test of hipness, which features the captains of heavy metal (all of whom could use a sprinkle of androgen on their Captain Crunch) standing in a pile of bones and blood and gristle, and looking every bit like the swing-shift crew at the local slaughterhouse.

What we're talking here is race shirts, or rather RACE SHIRTS in capital letters with flames coming out the back. That's right, race shirts. The pearls among swine of the T-shirt world, a runner's most highly coveted prize, and, quite possibly, the only clothing item in the world guaranteed for as long as the life of the owner.

I know what you're thinking: *This guy's kidding, right? I've got a second mortgage and two teenagers eating me out of house and home and he's worried about someone getting into his underwear drawer?* Contrary to what you think, this is no small problem—it's more like an industrial-size one. A pilfered T-shirt collection is the runner's equivalent of a pulled hamstring, a letter from the IRS and a flat tire on the Nimitz freeway. It's like catching the swine flu the day before the Boston Marathon. It's Hell On Earth.

I should know. I'm a victim of this tragic crime.

Imagine the shock when I came home to find my wife doing her aerobic step workout in my highly prized Spring Valley Marathon shirt. It was as though my face was held together by a number of unseen bolts, and each of them had suddenly been loosened a turn and a half. Everything sagged at once. She was actually sweating. In *my* T-shirt. Repulsive, man, *reee*-pul-sive. At that moment, even a zombie lurching through the night would have seemed pretty cheerful compared to the existential horror of that scene.

"Linda!" I shouted. "You've got my marathon shirt on!"

"Gee," she said, "I didn't think you'd mind. My shirt was in the wash and..."

"That shirt is from my untouchables collection," I said. "And that collection is off limits to everyone in the house." A rule I thought I had long before spelled out so plainly that even an innocent 4-year old could have divined its meaning.

"But you have so many T-shirts," she said. "The guest room is so full of them there isn't room enough to accommodate a proper clutch of dwarfs."

She was right. I did have an abundance of race shirts, yet I couldn't bring myself to part with any of them.

"That's not the point," I said. "Each one is a *special shirt*," I put a lot of English on the *"special shirt,"* stretching the "special" and spiking "shirt" with a sizable shot of air pressure against my larynx. I was compelled to go on laboring the subject like a man tied to a runaway cannon. Losing one shirt is as bad as losing an entire collection. I pointed an accusing finger at her. "And you've gotten sweat all over that one."

"You're a living, breathing prefrontal lobotomy," she said. I wasn't listening. In my mind bitterness perched like an ill-natured owl, blinking vengeance. "Listen," she added, "tomorrow I'll run over to Sport World and get you a new shirt."

"Ha!" The laugh caught in my throat like a kernel from the bottom of a popcorn box. Sport World clothing had an air about it usually associated with racket sports. Their T-shirts could suck the soul out of James Brown.

"Mother always said, 'Forever distrust a man who celebrates anything too much,'" chided Linda.

"I don't celebrate T-shirts," I said, skating up to the edge of the lie but not quite over it. I just kind of...commemorate them. Each shirt symbolized a certain race, a personal accomplishment. Like the Runyourbuns 10K, held on a day when I possessed true Olympic bravura. Propelled by either sheer fright or desperation, I ran a personal best.

I loved that race shirt the way little Timmy loved Lassie.

And the Holy Cow Half Marathon, where I violated my own precepts of running too hard too early and not drinking enough liquid along the way. The last five miles were a most unforgettable experience.

I was planning on having that shirt bronzed.

And the Bedford to Button Lip 40-Miler where my feckless and flat-footed attempt yielded not the possibility of winning, but only the bitterly wounded yet sweetly desirable promise of simply finishing.

I cherished that shirt the way the Baptists cherish Revelations.

And there was the Flat and Fast Eight-Miler, an erroneously named race held on a route that when graphed looked like a seismograph's representation of heavy aftershocks.

That shirt deserved to be kept under lock and key.

My paralysis broke and I leaped to my feet. "Those shirts represent battles fought and won," I said, storming about the room, my finger slicing the air theatrically. "They represent bragging rights. And at least 100,000 miles on my knees."

"So what?" she said. "When will you take the opportunity to wear one? When they do a Dewars profile on you? Those shirts are worthless."

The statement was a verbal slap in the face. My race shirts, worthless? The thought was a frightful one. If race shirts were worthless, then there was a nullity in the universe so great as to encompass the universe itself; the value of a person's life was nothing and his destiny, nothingness. The thought continued to sting and flay.

"Wait a minute," I said, hitting upon a dandy rebuttal. "What about your grandmother's dishes? When was the last time you took them out and used them?" Ah-ha! Trapped in her own argument. She would never set the table with grandma's china. It was too precious. I had untouchable shirts—she had untouchable dishes. And that was that.

"Not so fast," she said, throwing me a look you could iron clothes with. "Those dishes will be handed down to our children. Will you leave your T-shirts to them when you're taken out of the picture?"

I made a face at her euphemism, which sounded like something an insurance agent might say. But her question was a good one. What should I do? Did I want the kids to inherit my race shirts? The prospect filled my stomach with dread, like a huge football. I pictured our son, Tyler, using my cherished Waco Valley Invitational shirt to wipe down his motocross bike after a way-beyond-intense day in the mud. I saw our daughter, Emily, using my sacred Run for Fun 5K shirt to check the oil level in her car. I saw our dog, Lucky, chewing his mangy hide on a bed made of my shirts. The horrors of the Inquisition were nothing compared to the fate my mind imagined for my beloved T-shirts.

Suddenly, I went as limp and pliant as a green weed beneath streaming water. "Okay," I relented with a hoarse catch in my throat. "You win."

So the subject was dropped, but not forgotten. At least by me. Out of this small drama of frustration a valuable lesson was learned; it's an imperfect world. My race shirts will never be completely free from harm. And other than lose one to the wolves now and again (as even the best shepherds will), all I can do is grin and bear it.

But maybe in the Happy Running Grounds in the sky, where we'll all eventually gather for the Moses Marathon or the St. Peter's 10K, things will be different. With all those unemployed locksmiths and peace officers up there in the Great Beyond, it's a pretty sure bet that my T-shirts will finally be safe.

That must be why they call it heaven.

A GU Runner

Yes, I am running faster these days. Thanks for noticing. You're very observant. How much faster? Knocked ten minutes off my marathon Personal Record. No, not since last year. Since last week. I'm running better than ever, no doubt about it.

Yep, thanks to that new high-energy food: GU gel.

Eat it before each race? Oh, no. I eat it all the time.

It's not one of those silly fad foods. Just simple, common sense nutrition. At 100 calories per packet, 25 grams of carbohydrates, no fat or protein and a little jolt of caffeine from kola nut extract, what more could a body need?

How often do I eat it? Continuously. GU is the perfect food for active athletes. You don't have to chew, just rip open a packet and swallow the contents. I bite open hundreds of packets each day. It's not that difficult. You develop proficiency. I've increased my molar strength about 400 percent. Just yesterday I bit "The Club" off of a steering wheel for a motorist who lost his keys.

A bland diet? GU? No way. Hey, you inhale 20,000 liters of the same old air every day and never complain, don't you? You never hear anyone say, "I'm tired of this Arizona air, I could sure use some Ohio oxygen."

Besides, GU comes in a wide variety of flavors which helps you cover all the essential food groups. There's Vanilla Bean flavor, and vanilla is a vegetable, isn't it? With Orange Burst you get all your vitamin C requirements. With Tri Berry you get a daily allotment of fruit. With Chocolate Outrage you get lots of those good chocolate carbohydrates. And with Just Plain GU you get...well, you get something.

Or if you're feeling crazy, you can mix the five flavors.

Whattaya mean, those are chemicals that simulate the flavors? What are you, some kind of conspiracy theorist? Some kind of FDA watchdog?

If those were chemicals I'd be dead by now. I've eaten over a million packets of GU. Look at me, have you ever seen anyone healthier? The average cholesterol count is 200, mine is 12! You could drive a Tonka Truck through my arteries. The only fat I have is in my hair follicles and I think you'd agree that those are much slimmer.

I don't mean to preach here but, believe me, life is easier. Meals used to take a long time to prepare. Do you have any idea how much time the average person wastes deciding what to eat? I used to spend hours just coming to terms with dinner. Should I have chicken? No, I think I'll have pasta. Wait, I had pasta last night. I'm in the mood for Mexican.

Now? I don't even know when dinner is. Life is one continuous intake of GU enjoyed on a subconscious level, kind of like shopping mall music.

And forget about ever hitting the wall again. Forget it! With GU you get a truck load of sugar and caffeine. Sure, it makes you hyper, so you run a few more miles. A few more miles are good for you.

Personally, I run about 50 miles a day. It's kind of a necessity. Whenever I stop, I begin to feel like a Rolodex that's about to flip off into hyperspace.

Anyway, I gotta go. It's my lunch hour and I need to put in a few hundred laps around the office building. After that, I'll probably run in place beside my desk. Then I'll get a 30 miler in this evening. And maybe another 10 miles of speed work on the track. Care to join me?

Here, have a packet of GU.

Runners Anonymous

Hello. My name is Tim.

Hello Tim!

And I'm a compulsive runner.

[embarrassing silence]

I haven't run for, let's see now...eight hours.

All right! [wild applause]

This is my first Runners Anonymous meeting and I'm kinda' nervous. I'm not sure what to say, so I guess I'll just start at the beginning.

I got my first pair of running shoes about 10 years ago. Everyone else already had them. Lots of people were into distance running. It was the thing to do. A few of the guys I hung around with were into the hard stuff. We called them streakers, because they had consecutive days of running numbered, not in weeks or months, but *years*. One guy had a 15-year streak going.

[gasps of disbelief]

But I was strictly a social runner. It helped me stay mellow, you know?

[nods, mutterings of assent]

Then I got hooked up with a running club. There was a lot of pressure to get involved, to become part of the group. Someone was always asking me to go for a run. I couldn't say no. The next thing I knew, I was up to 100 miles a week.

Oooohh! [a woman faints]

After that, I got hooked on racing and my wife left me. Who can blame her? I was never home. I was doing everything I could find: local 10Ks, out-of-town half marathons, you name it.

Before long, I stopped showing up for work and lost my job. But I didn't care. My body fat was down to 3.2 percent. My cholesterol level was 126. I was flying high on personal records. I discovered ultra-running and my downward slide continued. Doing 200, 250 miles a week was nothing for a junkie like me. I'd get up in the morning and go on a 30-mile run just to jump-start my heart. I was living entirely off of endorphins. I guess I got depressed. I stopped coming home. I finally got evicted from my apartment.

No! I can't stand it! [a man bolts from the room]

Broke, homeless, desperate, I had to find some way to support my habit. Huddled beside a high school track one evening, I watched a runner circle around. I was insane. I couldn't control myself. "Hey, sweetheart," I hollered out, "interested in a little speed?"

"What's it going for on the street?" she asked.

"Cheap," I said. "A pair of used Reeboks and a bottle of Cytomax."

"You're under arrest," she yelled, twisting my arm behind my back and pinning me to the track. How was I to know she was an undercover running cop?

In jail, surrounded by hardened criminals, I knew I'd hit rock bottom. I'd lost my wife, my apartment and my job. And somewhere along the line I'd also lost the chest strap to my heart rate monitor. I began to weep.

That night I had a dream. A strange man came in and stood beside my bunk. He was wearing shorts, a singlet and a seeded number from the New York City Marathon. "Tim," he said, "it's Alberto." As he spoke there seemed to be a glow about him.

"Alberto," I gasped, "what are you doing here?"

"Everything will be fine," he said. "You just have to cut back on your mileage a little. No more than two workouts a day, understand?"

"You're right!" I cried. "I see where I've gone astray!"

The next morning, after they let me out of jail, I walked the streets and thought about the dream. Then I found myself outside of this building. A sign on the door said, "Runners Anonymous meeting in progress. Come on in."

So, that's my story. I know I have a hilly road ahead of me, one full of headwinds, potholes and angry dogs. But I swear, I'm going to take it one mile at a time. From now on, my splits are going to be positive, and I'm off speed for good!

[cheers, standing ovation]

Running In A Rut

I can't tell you what time I'll be running today, but I know that my next-door neighbor, Tom, will be hitting the street at exactly 5:30 a.m.

How do I know this? Because Tom is in a rut, albeit a satisfying one.

Tom gets up at 5:00 a.m. every morning. I see his light come on from my bedroom window. His kitchen light flicks on at exactly 5:05 a.m. I know what comes next. By 5:25 a.m. he is outside on the front lawn, stretching. I can—and often do—set my clock by Tom. At exactly 5:30 a.m. he is running. Tom goes for a 10-mile run on the same course he's used for the last five years. He warms up at a nine-minute pace for the first mile, an eight-minute pace for the next three; the remaining six miles he runs at a seven-minutes-per-mile pace. His workout never varies, not one iota.

"Any change is bad," Tom declares. "Ruts are what allow you to get good at something. If I do the same thing over and over, it becomes ingrained in my mind—running becomes a ritual."

I suggested to Tom that it might sound better if he said, "Some change of habit is bad." He looked at me as if I had just put on a Nazi uniform and goose-stepped into the room.

In running, all change of habit is bad.

I used to be comfortable getting my workout whenever I could find time or, like most people, if I could find a vacant spot in my busy day. I've run at dawn and with a flashlight at 2:00 a.m. I would get impatient with partners like Tom who wouldn't change their workout plans when a better one came along.

Now I'm the one who has a set time to run. I've allotted a two-hour period in the afternoon specifically for running and nothing else.

Why the change of heart?

Like Tom, I'm in a rut. And a rut is a ritual that is working for you. I've discovered that in order to become a more consistent runner, I've had to develop a running habit.

I never thought I would be so pleased to have a rut. It reminded me of the day a teacher pointed out to us that we always sat in the same seats, though we could sit anywhere.

Embarrassed, I tried for a few days after that to sit in the back or by the door, but I wasn't comfortable and was soon back in my old chair in the second row.

I have begun to cling pathetically to my ruts, especially the ones regarding running. My family expects me to march out the door at exactly 6:00 p.m. every evening, rain or shine. When I don't, they stop everything they're doing and holler: "Hey, dad, you're missing your run!" or "You're falling out of your rut!"

Finding Time To Run

Attention runners! Have you been missing workouts because you're just too busy? Are you depressed about atrophying muscles? Worried about slow 10K times? Concerned because you've plowed through a dozen time-management books, and several Take Charge of Your Life Seminars, and nothing seems to help?

If you answered "yes" to any of the above, you may be a victim of that dreaded runner's disease known as "Time Famine."

Bad news? You'd better believe it. Who can afford to miss a workout? Every runner knows that inactivity reduces fitness at a geometric rate more or less approximating the speed of light.

What causes Time Famine? Experts are baffled, but the latest theories postulate that this tragic disease is the result of bad time-use habits.

Is there a cure for this disease? You can complain all you want, you can shake your fist at the lowering heavens. You can even wonder what the Babylonians had in mind when they divided the clock into 24 hours. None of that will do any good. If you want to get back on the fast track to good running habits, you've got to get busy. This is the Jet Age. If you want to get things done, you've got to do them at 600 miles per hour, or slightly below the sonic barrier. And that means cutting corners. Here's how:

Personal Grooming: The rule-of-thumb for most people is one hour.

Want to be sharp, spiffy, with-it, up-to-date, fashionable, and still find time to run? Sorry. Can't be done. If you're fighting with your family for the bathroom the way Bill Russell and Wilt Chamberlain used to fight for control of the paint, you're wasting good time. Why stand in line just to get yourself worked up in a furious lather over uncapped shampoo when you could be getting in a few hill repeats? The same with shaving. How about brushing your teeth? Never mind the teeth. The teeth are all right. The looser they are, the more you can wobble them with your tongue. It gives the tongue something to do while you're running.

In this time of rampant posing, we runners must withdraw with dignity from the fray and simply never let our personal appearance make a statement. It just doesn't have a big enough vocabulary.

Breakfast: It takes about 20 minutes to eat breakfast.

No one ever died from skipping this meal, but if you insist on breakfast, make it something sweet and simple, like a Hershey bar or M&Ms. Or maybe a Hostess cupcake. You might remember from health class—if you weren't back there flipping ahead to the reproduction chapter—that a person is made of three things: his body, his mind and the part of him that thinks about eating sugar all the time. Victory isn't the only thing that's sweet.

Commuting: The national average is 30 minutes to and from work.

You can cut your highway time in half, and make your commute a combat adventure right up there with Jason and the Golden Fleece, simply by being a little crazier than your fellow commuter. Blink your headlights and honk your horn with great regularity. *Never* touch your brakes. Plow through red lights. Hurl *Road Warrior* epithets out the window. Pass trucks on the right. Playing Death Race 2001 in rush-hour traffic will get you to work in plenty of time to take a few laps around the office building.

Work: Based on a 1998 household survey, the average hours worked per week was 39.3.

Camus was mistaken about the myth of Sisyphus: it's not symbolic of life in general, just of our jobs. How do you free up enough time from your weekly income generating activity to fit in a run? It's difficult. Especially with a boss like mine. And especially if you want to pay the bills that come up every month, and will keep coming up, like teenage acne or nasal hair on a senior citizen. Quitting your job, however, is perhaps the best way to increase your mileage. After all, the quickest way to get back on your feet is to simply miss a couple of car payments.

Housekeeping: Two hours minimum says *Good Housekeeping.*

My argument against cleaning house is anthropological. The definition of dirt varies greatly from one culture to the next. In societies where people live in homes with dirt floors, they don't consider that dirt. Why should you?

It's a waste of time to clean house, especially if you've got children. Cleaning your house while your kids are still growing is like shoveling the walk before it stops snowing. Take a more lax attitude toward housekeeping. Let the mold grow in the shower stall. Permit the dirty dishes, pots and pans to accumulate. Forget the damp bath towels and dirty socks. Put up with the dust balls the size of tumbleweeds under the bed.

If your friends complain, just say, "You'll have to pardon the way everything looks, I'm a runner."

Pets: According to the SPCA, dogs and cats need at least one hour a day of brushing, petting and walking.

Ridiculous. Our little furry friends are perfectly happy with things just the way they are. In fact, they're probably overjoyed. I mean, have you ever stopped to wonder what your pet must think about you? You leave the house and come back an hour later with this amazing haul—chickens! pork! steaks! They must think you're about the fastest hunter on earth. What pet wouldn't be overjoyed having you as a master?

Go on, take a run. Rover would want it that way.

Time with your spouse: Ask any psychiatrist, psychologist or witch doctor and they'll tell you that you should spend three hours a day with your spouse.

Ask me, and I'll tell you that's *way* too much time.

You must remember, your spouse is not just an extension of you—she has her own life, her own problems. Her own tanning schedule. Spend time together? Hah! You're probably doing her a favor by not bothering her!

In those rare scheduling quirks when your paths do happen to cross, just make sure it's a genuinely affectionate time.

You might ask him out to dinner. He might be on his way to a track workout. He might suggest the following night. You might have a 10K scheduled. You might ask if Saturday is open. He might be going to a runner's workshop. He might ask what you're doing Sunday? You might have an out-of-town race. You might end up by giving each other some money, and then going out to dinner whenever you get the chance.

Ain't it all just too romantic?

Time with your kids: Two hours a day, according to someone who probably doesn't have children.

How long has it been since you spent some time with your kids? Go on, sit down with them, watch a little *MTV*. Help them with their algebra homework (What is algebra, exactly? Isn't it those three-cornered things?). Listen to them pepper their conversations with *awesome!* as they talk of skateboards. Now, after your eyes are glazed from all that parenting, ask them if they'll go for a run with you.

Hah! Are you kidding? Go for a run? With *you?* They're mortified to even be seen in public with you!

There are two ways to deal with children:

- Have all requests for parental attention registered on a piece of paper attached to the refrigerator by a magnet: *Mommy will be out running, but Daddy will be home, although he claims he plans on being grumpy tonight, so all kids steer clear.*

- Give them an American Express card at age 5 and send them on their way.

Eating dinner: One hour.

In most runners' homes, dinner is usually an industrious affair where much precious time is wasted. Learn to eat like a runner, and you'll be in and out of the kitchen before you can make a positive ID on the refrigerator. There are several things to keep in mind, however.

Don't worry about how food tastes. Being a runner is, in many respects, like being a Buddhist monk. You have to learn to eat without pleasure or distaste. Fortunately, bologna, cheeseburgers, beer and potato chips provide all the daily nutrients runners are known to require.

Don't get interested in food preparation. You're a runner, not a cook.

Learn to inhale your food according to aerodynamic principles, pressure differences and intake velocities.

Use the free time for a few wind-sprints in the front yard.

Spiritual Development: One hour.

My idea of God is different. Since spiritual development is, according to most, an individual thing, I see no reason why God can't be a runner. The God I envision wears a long white beard, singlet, shorts and a pair of Nikes. He sits on a big throne in the clouds and talks in a voice like Orson Wells to the tenth power, saying things like: "DID...YOU...RUN...TODAY?" Sound silly? Not really when you think about it. Sometimes isn't a good run almost a religious experience? And when you accidentally run into a telephone pole or a parked car, don't you see a lot of pretty stars in your head?

If you ask me, that's enough transcendentalism to drive even a cave-dwelling Tibetan holy man insane.

Sex: One hour, according to Dr. Ruth.

If you want a sure-fire way to free up time in this department, you can take a vow of chastity. You can become a nun or a priest.

You can. I'm sure not going to. Here's why.

I had a friend once who swore to God he was going to give up sweets. A couple of days later he ate a Snickers candy bar. Right after that, all his teeth fell out! Take a vow to give up sex? Are you kidding?

I think I'd rather take a little time off from running.

Some Days

Some days are just not made for running. From the crack of dawn to the last light of day; whatever the season, whatever the reason, nothing seems to go right. No one is sure what causes such days, but when they happen, you resist getting out of bed and set your heels against another workout. When you are finally forced to get up, either by thirst, hunger, bladder or guilt, you find that the day is just as lousy as you knew it would be.

On such a day it's impossible to locate your watch, your shoestring breaks, and old injuries mysteriously act up. Your kids put Icy-Hot in your shorts and live frogs in your shoes. This is the day the cat chooses to have kittens on your warmup clothes and your housebroken dog wets on your favorite T-shirt.

Times such as these seem very unjust.

On such a day you step on the bathroom scale and discover that you're 10 pounds overweight. You're also suffering from a cold or whatever it is that's going around; your sinuses are aching and you've got a hideous itch down in your ears in a place where Q-tips can't even reach.

Intense desire to weep. Sense of hopelessness.

On such a day you stumble over a footstool, almost breaking your leg, and curse every piece of furniture in the house. Your normally good-natured spouse is about as approachable as a whirling buzz saw, and any attempt to strike up a conversation yields only a sour glance that could bend steel nails out of plumb.

The morning is as layered as an onion, one strangeness on another.

On such a day you run out of breakfast cereal. All that's left in the house is a box of your kid's Cocoa Crunchies, a cereal with 18,395 calories and one vitamin per serving. A cereal so artificially sweet it could give bladder cancer to mice.

After breakfast you glance outside to see what the weather is like. Not that it really matters, for if it's a sunny day, it will be too hot for a run, and if it's cloudy, it will undoubtedly be too cold.

At times like this, angst seems to come in packages, a dime a dozen. Forty percent off the large economy despair.

On such a day the newspaper is filled with doom and gloom: Floods. Fires. Famine. The Incredible Shrinking Paycheck. A canceled marathon! Still, you're determined to go for a run. You slip on your shoes, pull on your

33

jacket and rush out the door...and you've forgotten your keys! You slump ashamedly back to the house and crawl through the bathroom window, knocking over a vase in the process.

Pretty soon they'll be measuring you up for one of those canvas coats you wear backwards.

In spite of every logical instinct you've ever had, you decide to give it another try. You step back outside and it begins to hail. A stone in your shoe migrates exactly to the point of most pressure. A strong wind blows in your face no matter which way you turn. And the neighbor's nasty little dog charges as if it means to dismember you, piranha-fashion.

On such a day you reach your limit. You decide that, more than anything else, you need to relax, unwind and forget your problems. And that's why instead of giving up and heading back into the house, you still go out for your run!

After all, on such a day isn't it just about the best thing you can do?

The Forgetfulness Of The Long Distance Runner

This is about a group of runners too long ignored by the running community, a group that suffers in silence because others have chosen to ignore our plight. This is about runners who can't remember splits, PRs, finishing times or anything else that requires the memorization of numbers.

Who are we? We're the ones who forget how fast we ran a 10K the day after it happened.

We're the people who, moments after finishing a marathon, give you a quizzical look when asked if we ran negative splits for the last half of the race.

Because we have forgotten.

As you can imagine, this causes us a great deal of humiliation and emotional distress.

Because somewhere in the not-too-distant past we probably ran a 10-mile race and said something like, "Wow, one hour and 25 minutes. That's a PR I'll never forget!

But 10 seconds later—WHOOSH!—the time is completely erased from our memory.

And rather than suffer the profound embarrassment which comes with stammering: "I, uh...Gee, I, um, seem to have forgotten what my time was," we try to put one over on you.

So instead of our finishing time, we'll say something like, "Where do we pick up our T-shirts?" or "Have they got any of those fruit bars left?"

Those of us who can't do the math are young and old, black and white, from every socioeconomic class and political persuasion.

What unites us is our profound shame at having to constantly nudge our wives or husbands, our boyfriends and girlfriends, and say: "What was my time again? Quick, I forgot."

Right now, medical science offers little hope for a cure.

No national telethons exist for people like us, where sweaty, exhausted entertainers weep gratefully in front of the TV cameras at each new pledge of $10,000 earmarked for research into this malady.

We don't meet every second Tuesday of the month in drafty church basements to pour out our stories in front of fellow sufferers perched on metal folding chairs while Danish and coffee are served in the back.

Instead, each of us develops our own methods for coming to terms with this affliction.

Mostly, though, I don't handle things well. When someone asks me to use an equation to determine my predicted marathon time from my current 5K time by using the equation M time = 5K x 9.489, I'm immediately engulfed with a sense of panic. I glance around to make sure they're not filming one of those "Stay in School" public service spots.

Then my brain lurches into action, frantically scans through the files of every math class I've ever taken and, as usual, comes up blank.

At this point, I hear myself saying in a thin voice: "Oh, uh...."

The voice eventually trails off. This is followed by a moment of strained silence until my brain flashes a frantic message ("No clue! No clue!"), and I hear myself saying weakly: "Huh?"

Mortifying? Oh, you betcha.

So what are we calling for here?

We're calling for a little tolerance, that's all. We're calling for understanding from our fellow runners who have no trouble summoning times, the understanding that maybe our brains can't recall finishing times.

Or PRs.

Or mile splits.

You don't have to rub it in.

Ten Things...
For A Runner To Do On Valentine's Day

1. Take a day off from running. Then take her out to dinner at a swanky restaurant. Order a nice meal, a bottle of Dom Perigon and try to stay awake. Do you know how frustrating it is to go out with someone who falls asleep before the main course?

2. Let go of the past. He dumped you three years ago. Doing 100 laps around his house every February 14th won't bring him back.

3. Buy her an expensive pair of shoes. Think of all those romantic long runs you can take her on once you've fitted her feet into a comfy pair of Nikes.

4. Visit him in the hospital. You clearly said a nod at a traffic light meant "all clear." Okay, you forgot to nod, but it's not your fault the bus driver didn't see him sprinting across the intersection.

5. Promise to spend less time training. Two workouts a day is excessive. She's beginning to think you're meeting someone on the sly. Besides, you know the only way you're going to improve your 10K time is by going to the track.

6. Buy some swank clothes. Which means, anything with long sleeves or pant legs. Just don't be surprised when she says: "Gee, honey, I hardly recognize you with all your clothes on."

7. Honor her with flowers. Lavish her with chocolates. Write her a love poem. Put down that log book and get busy. And avoid trying to rhyme words like run and fun, or race and pace.

8. Bring him breakfast in bed. The trick is catching him before he sets off for his morning run. For a classy touch, try a sachet of fruity sauce instead of the usual GU packet.

9. Have a romantic night at a top hotel. Don't choose a town that is hosting a major marathon. Don't use the time to taper for your next race. And for goodness sake, don't invite your running friends along to split the cost of the room.

10. Propose to her. Propose a trip to Boston on April 20th. Feed her a light breakfast. Take her on a romantic bus ride to Hopkinton. Then tell her you didn't bring enough money for the 26.2-mile bus trip back to the hotel. Trust me, she will never forget the gesture.

On-On!

If you're looking for a story about purer-than-pure running aficionados or the politically correct world of amateur athletics, forget it. This story contains no such beauty. It has no running philosophy by George Sheehan, no enchantments of the open road by Joe Henderson. There are no training tips by Jeff Galloway around which it revolves.

This is a cheap and tawdry tale of a beer quaffing, b.s. slinging gathering of runners. Period. That's all I can promise you. I apologize and understand completely should you choose to abandon the whole thing right here.

This story takes place along a brush-covered trail near Spokane, Washington. The event is the Inland Empire Run, an officially "unofficial" seven-mile run sponsored by a local chapter of the Hash House Harriers, a running club whose motto is: "If you've got half a mind to run with us, that's all you need."

The Hash House Harriers do not surrender themselves easily to mere description. They are called everything from "a group of politically incorrect runners" to "beer drinkers with a running problem" to "insane, debaucherous, drunken hooligans." Their behavior is *waaaay* out there, to be sure, but to many runners, like Lewis Giles, the Harriers spell instant stress relief.

"When I started running, I had the competitive bug," says Giles, a hasher from Lakewood, WA. "I raced for years. Then someone introduced me to the Harriers and my running changed overnight."

Giles explained that unlike other running events, a hash doesn't leave you frazzled. It doesn't leave you feeling like a downed power line in a storm. In a typical hash, runners follow a marked trail that may lead in any direction at any time. A hash has beer stops, whistle checks, flour marks...but no racing. One never, *ever*, races during a hash run. That is, unless one is trying to beat Dr. Kevorkian out of his fee.

"It's all about having fun," says Giles. "Most hashes are small and intimate. Some areas, like Los Angeles, attract 200 to 250 people to each run. But most hashes fall in the realm of 20 to 70 runners."

Hashers have many bad habits which help to define them as admirable and lovable human beings. Take, for instance, F.C. (short for F***ing Crazy), a Seattle-based engineer, and the merry prankster of the group. Like most hashers, F.C. is opposed to running with a chronic, harried sense of urgency. He does not believe that exercise is to be accomplished with a poor attitude in a mean back alley of life.

There is Doug Drury, the group's religious adviser, from Calgary, Canada. You won't find Drury attending biofeedback workshops, grief clinics or yogaholics. Nor will you see him centering, fasting, rolfing, grounding, channeling or colon-cleansing. He's too busy having fun.

There is Urinal Diver (a plumber), Fly Me (an airline hostess), High Beam (a large breasted woman), and a fellow named Na-Ke-Di-Sto-Li, which translates to Dances With Beer. Forty like-minded fools in all who will soon be running and laughing like college freshmen besotted with upside down margaritas.

"Do you bunch or fold?" F.C. asks each runner in the group.

"I'm not sure," says one man.

"We'll find out on trail," says F.C.

"Hashers away!" At those words the group accelerates up the trail like a dog with a winklepicker up its rear.

As the run progresses, I pick up the flour markings of the hash trail. Three dots indicate that I'm heading the right way. A little farther along, I see a quarter circle. Hashers call this a "checkpoint." It means that the trail could fork off in any number of directions. The idea is that those who reach the checkpoints first are most likely to veer off course as they try to figure out the correct trail.

While the faster runners explore, the rest of us have a chance to catch up. This is what sets hashing apart from other running events. It's great to be fast, but it doesn't get you much at a hash run.

At the first checkpoint I join the others as we scour the area for flour marks. Within seconds, I hear "On-on," the hashers' signal to indicate that the trail has been located, and, once again, we are off.

Hashing was founded in 1938 by A.S. Gilbert, a British officer stationed in Kuala Lumpur, Malaysia. Each Monday, after a weekend of heavy drinking, Gilbert would lead a group of British and Australian officials on a "hangover run" to purge out their systems. Afterwards, the group would settle into a local restaurant (a Hash House) for a large meal.

To make things more interesting, Gilbert and his friends patterned their run after an English children's game called "Hares and Hounds," where a "hare" marks a trail and the "hounds" take up chase. To add to the fun, the group would break for beer (a stop and top) at the halfway point, finish the run and head for the Hash House to chug down a few more cold ones. The post-run festivities, known as Down-Downs, became the source of many jokes, songs and ceremonies.

Sixty years later, the tradition of the Hash House Harriers has expanded to nearly every major city in the world. There are an estimated 100,000 hashers worldwide.

"There are some very competitive runners who hash," says Giles. "And there are some who see it's not a race and don't come back. It all depends on what you're searching for in your running."

As I amble up an impossibly steep hill, I'm searching for something cold to drink. Luckily, I don't have long to wait. A few minutes later, a shout of "Beer near!" echoes through the woods.

At the camp are several large coolers filled with beer. The group gathers and the area immediately goes from church quiet to shore-leave boisterous. We circle up to evaluate the run.

"No trees. No hills. A good, shitty run," says one hasher. "Too flat, too much asphalt, not enough asphalt, I froze to death and it was too hot," says another.

F.C., holding two beers, christens those of us who are "hashing virgins" by pouring beer on our shoes. Then comes the blessing: "*Aaaaaamen!* Drink it down, down, down...Drink it down, down, down..."

For the next several hours, hashers are singled out for various infractions. One man has been caught racing and is required to sit on a bag of ice and chug beer out of a running shoe. He drains the shoe while the group sings one of its signature toasts:

He ought to be publicly pissed on.
> *He ought to be publicly shot.*
He ought to be tied to a urinal,
> *to live there and fester and rot.*

A female hasher is put on the ice for the heinous crime of telling a bad joke. As she chugs her beer, the group sings:

She's all right,
> *she's all right.*
She's a little flat chested,
> *but she's all right.*

Next, a hasher named Gopher is given 12 seconds to drink beer from his shoe. He slams it down in six. Any beer remaining in the shoe must be dumped on his head. Gopher pours a little too much over his head.

"That's alcohol abuse," says F.C.

Another terrible joke is told. The guilty hasher is told to step forward and sit on the ice bag. The religious advisor pours the man a beer.

"I'll have water," he says.

Conversations stutter to a halt. Jaws freeze. The group looks embarrassed, flustered, put upon. They lean away from the man as if he were in the throes of delirium tremens.

"Water is ugly," says F.C. "We don't want water in the circle."

The group has been deeply offended. I imagine the man being secreted off in the night for shock therapy.

As twilight gathers, the group continues to fortify themselves with beer and laughter. Finally, F.C. closes off the circle with a lewd, but hilarious hash hymn, "Swing Low, Sweet Chariot."

The crowd begins to disperse when I realize that I've yet to fully understand hashing. What's it all about? There has to be a secret agenda, a hidden philosophy. But what? *What!*

I sidle up to F.C. and ask him why he thinks this beer-loving, bullshit-calling approach to competition is so attractive to runners.

"I don't know," he says. He looks away and then back at me, thinking.... "Because it's fun?"

Rent-A-Runner

I'm an ambitious runner. Each year I set my sights higher. I expect to do better than my rivals and, more importantly, my friends, and when I don't, I'm disappointed. That's why I often rent runners. Busy people, like myself, are sometimes forced to employ others to handle some of our "junk mileage." You should give it a try. The benefits are tremendous. For one thing, I can finish my workout in just a few minutes. For another, I don't sweat. Not a drop. I don't even get tired. In fact, after a rental workout, I feel better than ever!

Has it helped my running? Are you kidding? Since I started renting runners, I haven't lost a race. I'm as competitive as the papparazzi. I'm in great shape, too. My heart beats twice a day, once in the morning and once in the afternoon.

What's my 10K PR? That's none of your business. Let's just say it's *fast*. And then let's say it's taken a lot of money to get it that way. By my last estimate, around $895,000. That's because I use only the finest athletes: NCAA champs and USATF professionals. They're all quality runners, yes, but when stacked up against me, these guys are all sizzle, no steak. All pennies, no quarters. All doughnuts, no croissants. I'm the "Head Runner." They're just my employees. I have little in common with them, other than the fact that they run for me.

Some of my rentals I've found at races. Others are friends of friends. Most of them respect my authority and know their place in the pecking order, although I once had an underling ask to run with me. With *me!* Can you believe it? My advice to that guy was to go out and come back through the looking glass again. *No one* runs with the boss. The object of my running is to win races, thus the reason I can't be fraternizing with my workers. Besides, if I let my hirelings run with me, it would be like mud hens flying behind an osprey. When I run, it's pedal to the metal. Flat out. No prisoners taken.

I don't know the names of most of my rentals. I remember a few: Aouita...Plaatjes...Castro...Silva.... That's about it. If I kept track of every hired hand that came through here, I'd go bonkers. Why would I even want to? That's Komen's job.

Daniel Komen is my lead runner, the guy who reports to me. I wake up in the morning, pick up the phone, and I say, "Daniel, I feel like running 20 miles at a 5:30 pace. Go!" And he does. The man is as dependable as weekend rain.

From this point on I'm running, in the sense that an employee is running for me. Sometimes 400 to 500 miles of road work a week. Other times, a couple of hundred miles of speed work. You log that much mileage in your book without a little help and the next thing you know, you're coming apart at the seams; you've got to find a good tailor.

A note of caution: You can't just have rental runners lying around. You have to know how to use them properly. That's where good management skills come into play. Those who work for me are under strict orders to eat right, get plenty of rest and not enter races which might affect my training. This is something I insist on, up front. Being exempt from competition bothers some of my rentals but, frankly, what's needed here are worker bees and not more management.

As for my runners, I pay them generously (double time on race weekends and holidays), give them an excellent medical plan and unlimited access to the company masseuse. They get steady employment and I stay in shape. It's a good deal all around. Most of them say it's the best job they've ever had.

Why did I start renting runners? Good question. I guess one day I decided to go professional and asked myself, "Do I have the talent to take my running where I want it to be?" The answer was "no." So I hired Salazar. People always ask, "You mean *the* Salazar?" Truth is, I'm not sure. It might have been—it was definitely *a* Salazar. That much I do know, because I filled out his running schedule. And he had an impressive running resume, I recall. A fairly decent marathoner.

But what's important in good rental running isn't just the one note; it's the whole orchestra. So I shopped around. I picked up a German or two, and a bunch of South Africans from someplace I can't pronounce, and an Ethiopian and a half dozen guys who used to run for the Santa Monica Track Club. Next thing you know, I'm picking them up and putting them down like Forest Gump!

Oh, by the way, Komen hit me up for a raise the other day. I don't want him to quit, because if he does I will have to schmooze with dozens of runners before I find one to fill his shoes. I've decided to pay him an extra two grand a month.

Sure, it takes a lot of time, money and effort to remain competitive. I just don't want anybody saying I don't give 110 percent.

Tips From The Old Ones

Gather around. Many's the lore I have dispensed around the medical tent for those who have come to listen to tales of the Old Ones, the ancient runners who came before: Slow Twitch Ed, master of the ultra; Negative Split Dave, 10K specialist; Minimum Pulse Mike, marathon champion. Not ordinary athletes, but men who ran with superior confidence and form. A wild breed for whom fear was a chaperon and pain a mistress. Hearty souls who scoffed at sun block and laughed at cholesterol.

I have tips, yes, tips and observations, but with a manly gait, a rough-textured stride. Tips that are shocking, lawless, loud. Tips that can turn an average jogger into a real runner, a Greek mother's nightmare with hollow cheeks, veiny arms and no hips. Gather around, for I have tips.

Tip #1: Never stop running.

The Old Ones logged more miles in an afternoon than most of us do in a week. At night, they slept with their running shoes on and allowed themselves to dream only of negative splits. When they weren't sleeping, they were carbo-loading and drinking beer. When the sleeping and carbo-loading and beer were finished, they headed back out on the road and performed feats that are the stuff of legend.

Throw caution to the wind—or at least in its general direction. Learn to be obsessive. Instead of mowing the lawn, go for a track workout. Rather than attending a relative's funeral, go for a long run. Let your spouse worry about those nagging little details.

Tip #2: Wear old clothes.

There's no way to be polite about this part. Far better to strike to the heart of the matter and have done with it. Never wear cycling tights or those bright, eye-catching shorts. Such runners look like dweebs. Worse than that—they look like nerds, twits and egg-sucking geeks. The Old Ones wore ratty shorts and T-shirts that were 40 percent cotton and 60 percent food stain and sweat. And they preferred worn-out shoes. You should, too.

A good rule-of-thumb for proper running attire is: Do your shorts have enough rips and holes? Does your shirt smell so bad it makes your friends ill? If you answered "yes" to either question, you're well on your way to looking like a real runner. And remember, stay away from those scientifically designed, engineered and marketed ego-building shoes. A real runner wants fiery trials and ordeals. Old worn-out shoes are sure to provide them.

Tip #3: Eat right.

Forget what the hordes of self-righteous, tie-dye wearing, vegetarian nincompoops say. Boiled elderberries, tofu aspic, eggplant skins, organic carrots and spinach will not make you run fast. They will only make you hungry and eventually cause you to fade away like the Cheshire cat, leaving only a smile hanging in midair, or more probably, a gentle burp.

If you really want to run with supreme confidence and form, eat *real* food. Order your steak rare and well-marbled, lots of salt, potato on the side, extra sour cream. Roquefort on your salad. Brandy in your coffee. If you're on a road trip, eat at McDonald's or Burger King where you can get a lump of ground fatty meat fried in stale grease, topped with gummy yellow cheese and flaccid leaf lettuce, served on a floating sea of flabby fries.

And stop worrying about your health. After all, do you really want to grow old and develop systemic failure complicated by Alzheimer's disease, and spend your last years and the family fortune trapped in a nursing home, wetting your bed, drooling all over yourself and apprehending nothing? No, of course you don't. Much better to go out like Jim Fixx, in a blaze of glory.

Tip #4: Preach the merits of running.

Talk about your sport with the brisk eagerness of someone describing seeing a movie star at the grocery store, or witnessing a 20-car pileup on the interstate. Discuss running wherever you go. Bore your friends to tears. Watch their eyes glaze over as you describe, mile by mile, your last 50-mile run.

Lecture on the joys of sweating profusely, the feel of pavement under your feet, the sound of screeching tires when you dart through intersections, the high notes a vicious dog hits when a rock connects with its head. And don't forget to mention how every atom in the universe revolves around running. That's how everything stays together.

Tip #5: Fear no pain.

The Old Ones believed that suffering was its own reward, to be preferred to pleasure. Pain was pooh-poohed. If they pulled a hamstring, they didn't complain. They ran home and applied ice. If they ripped a tendon, they didn't baby themselves. They pulled their own teeth and lived with massive hemorrhoids. When an Old One had a heart attack, he took an aspirin and went to bed early.

Things haven't changed that much. Lots of runners get injured every year. How many? You don't want to know. The statistics, though, are glummer than a bellhop without a tip. But then, we're not talking a sissy sport here, such as bingo or badminton. We're talking running, where tortured quads, bent hamstrings and low biorhythms are a runner's companions. Remember, when you become a real runner, it's not a question of staying healthy. It's a question of finding an injury you like and sticking with it.

Summary.

I believe the Old Ones have spelled things out in sufficiently large block letters for even dairy animals to get a sense of their meaning. But in closing, here's one last thing to remember: Lust comes in many forms. For some it may be kicked off by a new automobile. Others might rise to heights of fevered yearning while shopping at the mall. The Old Ones preferred the stimulus that came from running around the clock. Like them, you should fear neither sweat nor public ridicule and make a point of traversing great distances daily. Make this your sole mission in life. Like a certain battery-driven bunny, you should keep going and going and going....

Pre: Another Sequel

So I'm out on the track in South Heaven doing my afternoon interval workout when the cell phone rings. It's Mort Weinstein, my agent. Once upon a time *my* agent.

"Pre!" he roars, as if it's been five minutes instead of five years. "Baby, what's shaking?"

"Lose the number, Mort," I say and toss the phone in the long jump pit.

An hour later, he's at the gate, leaning on the buzzer. Got a beard now. Shaved head. You can see where he had his horns removed.

"Look, Pre," he says, waving a folder, "I've got a new script."

"Been there, heard that," I reply.

"But this is great stuff," he cries. "It's a '70s kind of counter-cultural running flick. A burnt-out runner heads for the Olympics with his crazed lawyer partner and wins the 5000 meters. We'll call it *Fear and Loathing in Munich.*"

"No way, Mort," I tell him. "We've already done *Prefontaine,* the Disney movie and *Without Limits,* the Warner Bros. movie. That's enough."

"Enough?" he cries. "Do you think the public had enough of Eastwood after *A Fistful of Dollars?* Enough of DeCaprio after *Titanic?* Baby, we're just getting started here."

Same old Mort. Still pushing remakes, sequels and other lame scripts. Still weaving a fabric of b.s. so tight it could sustain the political platform of a national party.

"Forget it," I say. "Hollywood will never buy another running movie. Why don't you head back to your office and work on something new?"

"Something new? Great idea. How about *Pre Impact?* USA Track and Field hurtles toward the University of Oregon to release its frustrations on unsuspecting amateur runners. The public will take to it like a cowpoke takes to beans."

"No."

"How about *The Bowerman Show?* A track coach realizes that he has been melting rubber in his wife's waffle iron on live television. It's a sure-fire Oscar contender!"

"It'll never fly."

"*Jogzilla?* An unnaturally oversized monster of a runner shows up, and makes a beeline for Oregon, where all ambitious monsters go to prove themselves. Lots of mayhem and people getting stepped on."

"Absolutely not."

"Fontanic?"

"Mort, when you redecorated your brain room, you hung the pictures upside down."

"Run Hard With a Vengeance?"

"Good-bye, Mort," I reply.

"Wait. How about a TV movie? Four zany self-absorbed runners with weird hair styles put down one another and pass their time in mass petty bickering."

"You mean like *Seinfeld?*"

"No, like the '98 California gubernatorial debate."

"I've got to get back to my workout," I say, pushing him toward the gate. "Thanks for the visit."

"Hold it, Pre," he cries, reaching into his briefcase and yanking out a final script. "I've got an incredible idea! An absolutely spectacular concept! Something mind-blowing and original!"

"What is it, Mort?"

"It's a story about a mythic runner who can actually communicate with race directors: *The Race Whisperer.* Come on, sweetie, please! You owe it to me."

"I owe it to *you?"* I train the orbs on him and flip on the red beams. Mort takes off running. He still moves well for a guy with cloven hooves.

He's outside of the Heavenly Gate when he tosses a script over the fence, cups his hands, and hollers in my direction: "How about a running story set in England. We'll call it *Dog the Wags.* Whatda think?"

"Get outa here!" I shout back. But I can't help checking out the script. In it, I hammer a pack of English runners in the 5000, meet a double-scrubbed, peach-faced college student with long blond hair *and* my mug ends up on a Wheaties box.

I E-mail Mort and ask him to fax me a copy of the contract. Hey, what can I say? I've got this thing about movies with happy endings.

THE JOY OF RACING

Stories of wacky races and the anxieties and thrills of racing

The Race Management Is Not Responsible For...

Congratulations! You have decided to participate in the 10th annual Better Safe Than Sorry Marathon. But *caution*: the race management is not responsible for puddles, potholes, gravel, angry motorists, vicious dogs, free-range cattle and other vagaries of nature. Nor is it responsible for puddles, potholes, gravel, angry motorists, vicious dogs, free-range cattle and other vagaries of nature.

Run at your own risk: This event is physically strenuous and may cause fatigue, shin splints, tendinitis, heel spurs, plantar fasciitis, hypoglycemia and/or leg cramps.

Warning: Proper pace is encouraged at all times. Running anaerobically may result in side stitches, lactic acid buildup and DNFs.

Note: Your system may not tolerate the replenishment drinks offered at this event. Please check with aid station attendants before accepting fluids. If you become ill or nauseous, move to the side of the road immediately. Failure to do so may cause other runners to lose traction and veer off course.

Attention: Sunglasses can create visual "blind spots" which may cause you to collide with fellow competitors or immovable objects. In the event of a crash, remove your sunglasses and take immediate proper evasive action.

Important: Carry proper identification on your person at all times. Unidentified or unclaimed runners will not be recycled, rehydrated, reclaimed or returned to next of kin. If you believe you are a victim of a heart attack, stroke, seizure or drive-by shooting, please notify race officials as quickly as possible. Failure to do so may result in forfeiture of your official Better Safe Than Sorry Marathon T-shirt.

I have read and understand all of this. I am making this agreement and paying my entry fee in exchange for the privilege of competing in the event and using the stinky chemical toilets provided by the race.

Participant:_____

Parent or guardian if under 18: _____

Running Wild

"You've gotta run the Bay to Breakers...You have absolutely *got* to run the Bay to Breakers...I'm telling you, the Bay to Breakers is a race you don't want to miss," said Bob.

Bob Ornelas is my running partner and part owner of a brewery that makes some very fine beer. With my mouth full of his beer, I was obliged to listen to him expound at great length on the many wonders of San Francisco's Bay to Breakers race.

"It's a great race," he said. "A little looser than most, a little more kicked-back, but great."

"What's the course like?" I asked, dreaming, as I always do, of the possibility of medals or personal records.

"The course is perfect. You're gonna love it. Here, have another beer." Bob wasn't fooling me. I knew that the Bay to Breakers was a party kind of race, which is why he wanted to go so badly. Bob's a party kind of guy. He would attend the opening of an envelope. The Bay to Breakers didn't sound like my kind of race, but sometimes free beer can tip the balance. Having a zany friend like Bob can be a strain.

So I went to the race and it was not a pretty sight. It was a weird sight. There were more runners than I'd ever seen in one place. Over 100,000 runners. I don't think we were meant to lay eyes on so many of our own kind at once.

Bob and I had to line up *waaaaay* in the back, behind people dressed as trash compactors, tomatoes and high-rise buildings. One runner was wearing a full-length leotard of fire-engine red and a long cape of black satin. On his head were pasted black horns. What does a person have to do to get noticed in this town?

After the gun went off I lost Bob almost immediately. I got stuck behind a six-foot carrot, an Easter Bunny and a couple of tooth fairies. It took almost 30 minutes of jogging in place before I had even covered a mile. I'm a man of simple needs and complex carbohydrates. A clean start is one of those simple needs.

There were men and women pushing strollers and people being pulled along by their dogs. There were shopping carts filled with kids dressed as Teenage Mutant Ninja Turtles. Here was a race that needed an enema.

For the next several miles I was adrift in a sea of humanity. People were dressed to look like beer cans, running shoes and national monuments. And they were all walking around like dairy animals rather than acting like real runners. Take a hike! But not in front of me. A pack of Chesterfields and a bowl of Wheaties went by. Next I was passed by someone in a monkey suit. I tripped to avoid a centipede and spiraled to catch my balance. It was all Napoleon XIV stuff. Crazy, crazy.

Then, something, oh, kind of interesting happened. Just when I was about to throw in the towel and head back to the car, I fell in beside a woman with oiled-up muscles in a bikini that was so tiny it might have been drawn on with a Magic Marker.

After that, a woman wearing nothing but a smile came jogging down the street, rolling her body around like a cross between a cobra and a showgirl in a San Francisco porno act.

Well, okay, I can go along with this race. Not agree with it, perhaps, but accept it.

We crawled along for another few miles and I found myself almost enjoying the pedestrian pace. Especially with the snake girl beside me. Then the finish line came into view and a new energy seemed to fill everyone. Runners hollered and shouted. Cheering people lined the streets. The noise was incredible, like a herd of wild beasts thundering across the veld. The excitement in the air pushed those around me to a blistering 12-minute pace. Some of the runners crossed the finish line with arms raised high in the air, feeling the thrill, the exaltation of a personal victory.

Then the party got underway.

Food and drink materialized everywhere. One person was handing out cookies and yogurt. Someone else was giving away bananas and popsicles. Another kind soul was distributing Calistoga water. And, hey—bonus point—beer. *Free* beer!

All right, now we're talking Bay to Breakers!

So wouldn't you know it, an hour later, just as I was starting to enjoy myself, Bob came wandering up and took hold of my arm and bodily dragged me away. It was time to go home.

Glancing back, I said goodbye to the cookies and yogurt, bid adieu to the snake woman and waved a tearful farewell to the free beer. Then we got in the car and drove away.

Like I said, having a zany friend like Bob can be a real strain.

The Holy Race Director

Very early on, when I was a nobody in the running club, when people called me "you boy!" I realized that there are two kinds of people in this sport: There are those who race and there are those who direct races. Based on my experience in this regard, I have come to believe that the ability to placate the Holy Race Director is quite simply the highest form of civilized discourse, living proof that the human spirit can be beaten, shamed and trod upon and still retain a small amount of dignity. In other words, I don't blame brown-nosers. Some of my best friends are tuft hunters. But I also determined that when I finally grew wings and halo and became a race director, I would not demand such outright subservience from others. Never. No way.

The desire to remain plain, simple and above the common running herd has remained with me. Even though I now direct a number of races, I have remained incredibly humble. I don't need pilot fish swarming around me in order to bask in the glory of being a shark.

I will tell you, however, that it isn't easy to avoid being sucked up to. Let me give you an example. Last week, during the Tim Martin 10K, I was standing by the starting line digging into a fresh croissant when I noticed that something was wrong with my coffee, in the sense that it wasn't there.

"I don't seem to have received my coffee," I said to a nearby finish line timer. I didn't make a big issue of it. I just noted the fact. Perhaps my face betrayed some small sign of annoyance; a race director's coffee is supposed to be served with a race director's croissant, is it not? Within a minute, the caterer himself appeared at my elbow, bowing and shifting from one foot to the other, looking a little like the boy whose father has just arrived home to hand out spankings.

"Is there something wrong, Mr. Martin?" he whimpered.

"My coffee seems to be late," I observed.

"I'm so very sorry, sir!" he said, with a sort of gag-level genuflection as he rushed off to locate my coffee. Can you believe it? The peonage I'm forced to work with!

Another such instance of odious brown-nosing took place later in the day when I was forced to wait ten additional minutes for a runner to finish the race. The man appeared to have died and slightly decomposed on the course.

"I'm sorry, sir," he puffed, as he staggered across the line and I could tell from his inflection that he was trying to apply suction to my executive stature.

"I certainly hope you are," I said, leaning back in my director's chair until the struts popped and the chair gave evidence it just might fly apart. "I also hope you'll get your 10K time down a little before you come to another of my races." And then I hollered to Alex, my T-shirt operations manager: "No shirt for this guy. He's too slow." But I swear, I only had the finish-line captain kick the man once or twice to get him out of the way so my crew could disassemble the scaffolding.

Which brings me to another problem. Tony Lombardi, my official course marker, evidently did not read my book, *How to Put On a Great Race in Lots of Easy Steps*, when he went against strict orders and marked the course on the *left* side of the road instead of the right.

"But you told me to mark the left side," he mewed.

"I most certainly did not," I said in a steady and reproachful tone. And to offer proof (not that I need to—I did so only out of the kindness of my heart), I called over my personal race secretary, Karen Phelps, who has been around so long she can taste an organizational problem almost as quickly as I can discern whether the '65 Chateau Le Bleu I ordered during dinner was, in fact, properly stored and chilled. She told Tony that I most certainly had said to mark the right side of the course.

And Tony, who at his best displays all the dynamism of moistened zwieback, moaned his apology and fell to my feet, crying. I thought of telling him it was totally unnecessary to oil my oyster like that, but why hassle him? I'm too big for that. You'd better believe, however, that Tony's disrespect of authority was Subject Number One at the post-race meeting later that evening.

While I'm on the subject of blundering fools, I should tell you about Wanda Bazemore, my Number 2 aid station leader. While navigating deeper intellectual waters than is her wont, Wanda took it upon herself to serve my runners Cytomax in four-ounce cups instead of the regulation eight-ounce cups I insist upon. When I lectured her on this she sat small and still, her eyes peering up at me, looking like a rat in a soup can. Then she heaved in a great suction of air. "Who do you think you are? God?" she cried, both asking and answering her question in one breath.

Finally, gasping, trembling and weeping, Wanda begged my forgiveness and spent the next 20 minutes basically grooming my fur. Can you believe it? What I wouldn't give for a couple of honest minutes with someone unimpressed by my speed, authority and handsome Gore-Tex packaging!

The awards ceremony was something of a fiasco as well. Awards coordinator Charlie Perkins got so wrapped up in his duties that he forgot to mention me, the race director, the customary eight to ten times while distributing the medals. Sheesh! Several times I tried to signal Charlie, but he just looked at me like: duh. And that's not the worst part; the idiot forgot to award me my annual race director's trophy!

Sheesh! If ignorance were corn flakes, that man would be General Mills. I'll get through this, I told myself as I knocked over a course monitor on my way up to the awards platform to choke the life out of Charlie. I'll get through this, and when I do it will be the last time. I'll pay good money if I have to. I'll threaten. I'll bribe. But I'll never put up with such incompetency again!

Say Again?
Snatches of conversation heard at the Western States 100

At Squaw Valley (0 miles): Only 100 miles to go. *** Nervous? I started hyperventilating at four o'clock yesterday. *** I'm so uptight that if you plucked me, you'd get a high E. *** The hardest part of this race begins at the start and ends at the finish. *** I hear they don't expect anyone to finish. *** I don't compete; I'm just here to run. *** I feel like a rack of lamb about to be thrown to a turkey vulture. *** I'm not out to win, I'm out to finish. *** By the time you get in shape to run this race, you're too old to do it. *** The course is tougher than a two-dollar steak. *** The idea is to have a good time. If that's not possible, then the idea is to get really drunk afterwards and think you did. ***

At Robinson Flat (30 miles): No, I didn't stop. The leader flew by so fast it just looked that way. *** Check out all the food. There's enough here to feed the five thousand, without the miracle. *** They actually had a topless aid station, but they were all guys. *** I thought I was slow, but I passed a guy who looked like a monument. *** He said it was a secret drink that gave him instant energy, then he threw up. *** If you start to feel good, don't worry, you'll get over it. *** I didn't go out too fast, I just died too soon. *** Any idiot can run a marathon. It takes a special kind of idiot to run an ultramarathon. ***

At Last Chance (43 miles): I spilled PowerAde on my hands and my fingers have been stuck together ever since. *** Crying about how tired you are is like termites bitching about aluminum siding. *** I hate it when I drop out and the spectators applaud. *** I'd like to see this race regulated to the same vortex of oblivion where rotary phones go to die. *** Hills always look steeper just before you run them. *** I've got to find another port-a-tree. *** I wish there was more oxygen in these mountains. ***

At Foresthill (62 miles): I'm not lost, just confused. *** My wife thinks I'm out here having fun. *** I can live with rain and I can live with dust, but when I eat dust in the rain it ticks me off. *** She not only caught her second wind, but her third, fourth and fifth wind. *** Speed is sex, distance is love. *** It hurts up to a point and then it doesn't get any worse. *** Your feet look better without toenails. *** I didn't fall, I'm studying these deer tracks. *** Why couldn't this be a 100K? *** I never met a hill I couldn't walk. ***

The River Crossing (78 miles): I was doing good until I hit the fourth checkpoint for the second time. *** I thought he was sitting in the river to cool off, but when I ran by, I found out he was standing up. *** Is this the karmic caboose or what? *** There are worse ordeals, but at the moment I can't think of any. *** I swear, my IQ drops 50 points every time I lace up my running shoes. *** What doesn't kill me sure does make me hungry. *** If the bone's not showing, just keep going. ***

Highway 49 (93 miles): The finish is just ahead. *** It only hurts when I breathe. *** The X-ray will probably look like a jigsaw puzzle. *** I'm sick of the pain. *** They used more arrows than Geronimo and he still got lost. *** I ducked a low branch and when I looked up, I caught a face full of lumber. *** Trust me, this is the last hill. *** I just experienced a warp in reality, like in the Wizard of Oz, when the movie shifted from black and white to color. *** Don't quit now. *** This is a race written by the Brothers Grimm. *** Lack of sleep is the cheapest and most underrated hallucinogenic drug known to man. *** You're almost there. ***

At Auburn (100 miles): All *right!* *** A finish line never looked so good. *** What I really need is a decent burial. *** One hundred miles of roots and rocks and I tripped on my shoelace. *** I don't need that quick-energy stuff when I'm running; I need it when I'm driving home. *** Did anyone find a jog bra on the trail? *** You could translate Shakespeare's sonnets into Sanskrit in the time it took me to finish. *** I did it! *** Fast? I was passing rocks and trees like they were standing still. *** Any ultra you can walk away from is a good race. *** I reek like a roadie who's toured for a year with the Sex Pistols. *** Man, they should put me out to stud! *** Wanna do a cool down? ***

One For The Road

I must be getting old. Last weekend I actually had second thoughts about hopping in the car and driving 300 miles to an out-of-town race.

That's too far to go, I lectured myself. There's too much work to do around the house. Besides, you'll probably hit weekend traffic and end up driving all night. But it took me only a second to remember why I should ignore my own advice: Fast food, freedom and rock 'n' roll! And what awaited me: A new course, new competition and the chance for a new PR! Who in their right mind could refuse all that?

An hour later, the sun setting to the West, I was on the road heading for the San Francisco Bay Area.

"You're driving 300 miles just to run a race?" a friend asked. "Why on earth would you do that?" I got the same incredulous response from a fellow runner when I told him my plans. "Are you crazy? You're driving all the way down there? In the middle of the night?"

Granted, there are potential problems in attending out-of-town races; problems with the car. Problems getting to sleep. Problems finding the race site the next morning. And so on. Right—but those things can also happen in a race close to home. At least this way you get a new and unique T-shirt as you risk life and limb.

Besides, on a road trip everything seems so much better. Your Circle-K coffee tastes better than a latté. Your Dodge Dart runs like a Vinny Testarossa. And, hey, that may look like a Motel 6 you're staying at, but it's the Hilton! Most importantly, you're free, liberated. Away from people and work and all responsibilities. You can squint into the windshield and see down highways that travel on forever. Time dissolves.

If you're squirming already, splendid. This is strong stuff. It should have you searching for your car keys in a minute. In order to properly enjoy a road trip, you should always go alone. Once I made a mistake of taking a road trip with a friend and I spent the whole time pretending to be vastly amused by his stories, which I had already heard several thousand times over the desk, over coffee, over the course of the last few years. It was yak, yak, yak and chat, chat, chat until I wanted to 86 the guy. I wanted to ice him. Now I travel alone and I'll continue to do so as long as natural laws continue to hold sway.

There are other pluses that come with traveling alone: There's no fighting over radio stations, no irritation with spur-of-the-moment pit stops after copious ERG and Gatorade consumption, no whining when you choose to drive all night to get to your destination.

Music is indispensable to your well-being on a road trip. To be a truly great road-trip song, the music must be loud, have a strong beat and at least one dynamic vocal solo. Take your pick: "Fire Lake" by Bob Seger, "Lights" by Journey, "Don't Look Back" by Boston. Believe me, six hours of a steady rock beat will bring you to the starting line of your race feeling like the Red Hot Chili Peppers on an espresso buzz.

On a road trip you eat differently than you do at home. Barbecue chips lie on the seat beside you. Double-fudge cookies are stuffed into your cheeks until they are grossly distended. Burgers, french fries and shakes suddenly become definitive food groups. A pre-race dinner at Colonel Sanders? Go for it! On a road trip there's nobody around to check up on you.

Coming back from an out-of-town race is every bit as enjoyable as heading out on one. You've had a good weekend. A great run. You drive home with that plump, sassy, burnished glow that comes from a really big achievement, awash in a cyclone of race memories. You slip back into the driveway with rosy cheeks and an obnoxious surfeit of hope and good humor. And, if you're really smart, you greet your spouse with a hug and a kiss and a complimentary race T-shirt.

After all, you might want to go on another road trip next weekend. I guess I'm not as old as I thought.

Crash Course At Russian River

Ukiah, Calif., June 3, 1984—They began arriving before dawn, at first an early few and then in numbers so great their ranks threatened to spill out into the surrounding vineyards. Runners. Hoards of them—all converging on a desolate strip of blacktop in Northern California's Mendocino County, gathering in the repose of the Yokayo Valley for the sixth annual running of the Russian River Marathon.

I drove down the coast to join in the fun and to run what I hoped would be my first sub-3:00 marathon, the magic mark in every marathoner's world, a boundary whose other side beckons like the siren's song. A sub-3:00 finish had eluded me in two previous races, but I was confident to the point of certainty that Russian River would change all that.

A restless night in the campground hadn't dampened my spirits. Nor had an early 6:00 a.m. wake-up call (one of the special punishments of marathoning). My confidence had even remained unshaken through a frantic, last-minute search for the staging area. I had trained hard for this race; breaking three hours would be the easy part.

The whole idea was more seductive than it should have been. The simple fact is that when you run a marathon, it is seldom easy. My friends warned me not to become overconfident. I should have listened, but I didn't.

An amplified voice called us to the starting line. People stripped, stretched and pinned on numbers. Officials rushed back and forth, making last minute checks. My girlfriend applied Vaseline to my armpits (the extent of my pleasure for the day) and I took my place with the others.

The first rays of sunlight caressed the morning sky as the final seconds ticked off the clock. Runners fell silent. Heads were bowed as though in some odd sort of religious observance. Then the sharp crack of a starter's pistol pierced the air and the race was underway.

For a short time the large field of runners moved along in a tight knot. But the pack broke up almost as quickly as it had formed, the elite runners pulling away, the less conditioned falling back, and others, simply maintaining.

My breathing was labored for the first mile or so as my body attempted to find and settle into a steady state. By mile two, however, I began to loosen up. The going became fast and easy. My breathing settled out and my legs moved effortlessly beneath me. I allowed my mind to drift.

If someone asked you to sit down and design the perfect marathon course, you'd probably want to run it through the Yokayo Valley. As you move along the road, endless rows of grapevines promenade by, thinned by the morning haze. You delight in a bluster of plumb bushes. You marvel over the pink and white blossoms that adorn the fruit trees. The intense beauty of the 26.2-mile course is etched in the mind.

Making marathon pace is like making prose; it's an introspective business. A good marathoner always monitors body signals. Hydration and respiration are important. Heart rate and heaviness in the thighs and calves are to be followed. The internal questions should never stop: What was my time on the last split? Should I back off and save something for later? Concentrate on each step; know intimately every minute you are running a marathon.

I increased my speed, silently, confidently. The miles continued to tick off effortlessly. A vision danced in my mind: It was the final mile of the race and I had taken the lead. There was one runner close by, challenging me. He pulled alongside and it was a sprint to the finish. Spectators were screaming and cheering. I made a heroic surge...broke the tape...and won!

My fantasy was transforming itself into reality. Or at least attempting to. Oblivious to the 20 miles that lied ahead, I sprinted, surged and passed my more sensible companions. I ran like a man possessed.

It was a transcendental moment. My body became a celestial machine, gravity relented, and my shoes whispered across the road. A three-hour marathon became a piece of cake. I would knock 30, no, 45 minutes off my best time. As a runner I am willing to take on risk. There is nothing more empowering than taking a risk and reaching your goal. All runners must step toward the edge occasionally, some more often than others, some closer than others. Success in running often relies on a calculated gamble. We all do it.

But a problem developed; I ran out of energy before I did race. At the half-marathon turnaround, my legs suddenly felt numb and bloodless. My body began to quiver with fatigue, like a top that's begun to wobble.

In marathoning they call it "The Wall," that unmarked point in the road where familiar ends and unfamiliar begins. The Wall is a threshold of pain few care to traverse. It is that unknown quantity in all of us.

The Wall beckons you to experiment, much as you did in early youth. Can I leap off the high dive? Can I bike down the mountain with no breaks?

Can I run an additional 13 miles when my body is ready to shut down? As a child I had never been one for taking chances. Caution was bred into me. I never played with guns, or made a hobby of experimenting with pharmaceuticals, or flung myself off a cliff while clinging to a kite. Yet I was at a crossroads: to stop or continue....

A serious runner comes to think of fatigue as city residents do car alarms: You know that it's supposed to signify that something bad is going on, but you've heard it so many times you disregard its warning. My decision was to finish. The burning sensation in my legs would have to be endured. Besides, how much worse could it get? Forcing determination over my fear like a tight lid over a saucepan, I continued on.

By mile 14 the stinging sensation that had started in my legs had worked itself up through the rest of my body. I was serenaded now by a chattering internal monologue...Push hard, don't quit...Anchor those feet to the pavement. My brain sputtered out banal, mixed metaphors and burdened thought fragments like a cold car engine revving up.

At 15 miles I began to lose the ability to concentrate. My legs and stomach were cramping badly and I ran along clutching, grimacing and bending. My fears became greatly magnified. The instinct was to stop before things got worse.

To keep moving, I invented a mental ploy: I would imagine the finish line to be one mile away. When I completed that mile, I would try for another. I attempted to concentrate, to focus on each step, on every yard, but it wasn't working. I was in the grip of an inexpressible fatigue.

Tibetan monks were expressly trained in swiftness of foot for the purpose of carrying messages from one monastery to the next. It was said that they could run up to 300 miles in 30 hours. What enabled them to do so was a kind of disassociative cognitive strategy. They would gaze at a peak miles away and repeat their sacred mantra in synchronization with their respiration and locomotion.

By mile 18, I was a study in slow-motion disaster. I was slower than zombies playing Monopoly, slower than a nursing home sack race. I had hit the fabled marathon wall so hard I was having trouble navigating a straight line.

Inner doubts continued to nag me. Was I doing serious damage to myself? Would I be able to run again after this? Would I want to? I searched for a reason to keep going. I had plenty for quitting.

For the experienced marathoner the 20-mile mark is where the race actually begins. Competition is sized up, surges thrown in and the leaders begin to make their bid. For most marathoners, though, the last six miles are every bit as difficult as the preceding 20.

The 20-mile marker afforded me a slight amount of motivation. My mental state roller-coasted from elation to despair, my energy level rising and sinking along with it.

The sun inched higher in the morning sky, sizzling along its trajectory. The temperature rose along with it. Trees were like images burned in green flame. Road signs were bronze stamps inked and punched on my brain. The pavement became a bed of white-hot coals. The heat rose through my arches and legs and rekindled itself in my brain.

My pace faltered and I slowed to a walk. I felt immediately ashamed. Walking was only a step from stopping. And stopping was an unthinkable act. I became dizzy and lightheaded. A queasy feeling came over me. I felt as though I was about to collapse.

At 22 miles I entered a strange, uncharted territory of endurance. I was cast into a nightmare where I became a prisoner of my own determination, an instrument of my own destruction. I struggled along in a tumult of agony and despair, slipping in and out of a semiconscious state, oblivious to everything around me.

At 23 miles I was coming apart, melting like a spiraled Dairy Queen cone in the wind. My cells were liquefying. All I needed to do was apply a little more heat and I'd turn to steam and vanish, no more than a wispy memory above the vineyards.

The colors had begun to drain out of things; the world had begun to take on the dull, grainy qualities of a newspaper photograph. My body was sending notice that it had had enough.

In that long moment before your mind shuts down, your organs pump adrenaline, bringing you vividly to awareness, and you have a long, slow time to see with such relaxed precision. All at once you are perfectly behind your eyes and a true artist of seeing.

As I stumbled through the last aid station there was a sense of impending doom. I took water. I heard voices. The voices roused my sense of reality. The reality heightened my agony and I hit the boundaries of my endurance. The world went black.

It's a lot like dropping off the edge of the world or lifting the corner of the universe and looking at what's underneath. Pushing beyond your limits is to see into the dark heart of things. A glimpse into no-man's land between life and death. A short fall to the side of the road in the middle of nowhere.

I awoke in a flash of astonishment. It was over. Now there would be no shame attached to dropping out of the race. I had earned my ride the hard way. Voices came from above. Aid-station volunteers gathered around. A discourse over my condition filtered down. Opinions vacillated.

Astonishingly, I heard myself say, "I've got to finish. Help me up."

Strong hands lifted me to my feet. The fatigue unfurled slowly, like a creature waking and stretching after a long nap. I wanted to drop back to the ground, but instead I broke into a shuffle. A few hundred yards down the road the torment worked itself into another crescendo. Darkness loomed again. This time I knew what was coming.

I awoke slowly and came gradually back to the position from which I could access myself. I was somewhere in the Yokayo Valley, gazing up into a blue sky, still alive and intent on staying that way. I was finished for good. I would not move. I would lie still and patiently wait for the paramedics to sweep in and carry me off.

As the fever slowly left my veins, I heard a command: "Come on, get up!" To anyone else, the order might have been easily ignored; to a brain that had been folded, spindled and mutilated, though, it was something to note. I remember being perfectly dazed, first by the demand, and then by how damned unhappy the whole prospect of getting to my feet made me feel.

I turned my head toward the road. There stood a runner, bent over, hands on his knees. "Come on," he said, "we can finish together." As he spoke, his body weaved to and fro.

What powerful forces reignited a fire that was almost out, banked to near extinction by big doses of agony and fatigue, I'll never understand. I know only that his words were a healing salve, his determination a shot of adrenaline.

"Come on!"

My determination redoubled. Quadrupled. With all my will, knowing I must do it quickly or not at all, I staggered to my feet. The pain was so intense it defies description. I took his side and we moved off down the road, silently, conserving strength, pacing off one another.

Like Napoleon's numbed, dog-weary, demoralized soldiers, we jogged, walked and ultimately dragged ourselves toward our goal. I was blind tired, but the burden was shifted and the suffering pushed back by a common bond. Together, we rounded the final bend in the road, and there it was—the finish! I had never seen a more beautiful sight in my life.

Running is a sport that evokes wild swings in emotion, everything from elation to despair. I experienced the full range, all at once. I was overjoyed, exhausted, astonished, and I felt like dying.

I crossed the line, stumbled to the nearest shade, and sat there a full minute. Then I pulled myself upright and searched for my friend. I wanted to thank him. I wanted to share a cold beer and a laugh and relive the race with him. I wanted to compare experiences. But he was nowhere to be found.

I checked the finish chute, searched the crowd, scanned the parking lot. Nothing. It was as if he had simply vanished...or never really existed at all.

Real or not, I'll always remain indebted to that man. I've entered many marathons, but nothing since Russian River has given me such a deep awareness of my physical and emotional limits. You can come out of such an experience broken in mind and body, or you can come back whole and bring with you the knowledge that you've explored regions of yourself that, in most people, will always remain uncharted. I came back whole. And thanks to the runner at mile 25, I learned an invaluable lesson about friendship and camaraderie in the process.

Tears On My Asics

You'll have to excuse me if I sound a little morose. I am morose. So is my friend, Bob. He was crying when he called. Well, he didn't blubber or anything, but almost. Bob called to tell me that the Russian River Marathon has been canceled. Discontinued. The race is history. I'll tell you the honest truth, I felt low. Very low indeed. Bob and I are devotees of the Russian River Marathon. We've been running it for years. This was something that neither of us had expected.

"It stinks," said Bob. "Our favorite race bites the dust." Then I heard him blow his nose for a very long time. In fact, after a while it was pretty clear that he wasn't blowing his nose at all. He was trying to disguise the fact that if he were not so audibly clearing out his nasal passages, he would be weeping.

After Bob managed to pull himself together we relived a few old Russian River memories, turning over the good times like delicate fall leaves, one by one. After that, there was a deep, moist silence. Then Bob hung up.

People think runners are shallow and mechanical—put on the shoes, step out the door, run down the road—but we're nothing like that. Our feelings run hot and deep, especially where races are involved. Extra especially when the race is a marathon. The cancellation of a marathon is terrible, no matter how right and proper such decisions might be. This has always been true. It is particularly so for Russian River, the race that has touched me deeply in many ways.

To describe the Russian River Marathon I would have to take you to the Yokayo Valley in Mendocino County, California, and we would start running just as daylight was breaking. We would move along the road, scattering a covey of quail as we went, and I would say, "Look around you," and you would see rows of grapevines, pruned by the mist of morning. You would see fields of green grass and the pink and white blossoms that adorn the trees. Then I would say, "Breathe deeply," and you would breathe and remember the smell for the rest of your life, the rich aroma of a spring morning in the vineyards. A smell like milk and honey, perfumed with clean country air.

But it isn't just the beauty of the Yokayo Valley that makes the Russian River Marathon so appealing. It's the race itself. The history. The personal touch that every runner, race director and volunteer has ever put into the event. It's a little of my own history, too.

It was at Russian River that I first tried to break three hours in the marathon and failed miserably. Due to a brain error, a little valley of stupidity in the vast territory of marginal competence I have as a runner, I went out fast and faded early. Actually, I died. I'm talking full cortical meltdown. That was my first experience at Russian River. Thanks to my running partner, Bob, it wasn't my last.

Bob Ornelas is a character right out of the pages of a John Steinbeck novel. He has long hair, impetuous eyes and a scar shaped exactly like half of a broken Steelhead Pale Ale bottle (his favorite beer) across the bridge of his nose. He also has a great wild-card personality. Bob is a former Arcata city councilman, a conservationist, and the kind of guy who would drink a '59 Dom Perignon out of a "Big Gulp" cup. He is in touch with what's hottest in derivative *fin-de-siecle* pseudo culture. He was doing the Seattle grunge thing (wearing ripped and tattered clothing) long before it became popular.

Sometimes Bob gets angry with me. He rummages through my garbage can. (When are you going to start recycling?) He scolds me when I use household products like Windex. (Hey! This stuff is toxic!) And he hates it when I drink my favorite domestic beer. (Those slobs at Coors have unfair labor practices!) But I still love the guy. Why? He's a confirmed runner. A one-man orgy of high mileage and non-stop racing. Bob is also one of the few people I know who seems to have any fun in public. Not a day passes in his company without a little good-time commotion. Sometimes he's merely an innocent bystander, but not often. Bob is tethered with only the slenderest of strings to normal and well-socialized behavior. That's one reason I like him so much.

Another reason I like Bob is because he's the one who talked me into going back to run Russian River again. I'm glad he did. Otherwise, I might have missed lots of unforgettable memories, such as the Year of the Storm. There was terrible weather that year. It rained from start to finish. Thunder cr-r-racked and crashed and lightning licked the sky close enough to bounce us off the ground. Rain fell with an intensity that beggars the imagination.

And there was a strong headwind that seemed to blow in all directions. It was a cold, wet and miserable race, and everyone had a great time. All around us runners were laughing and shouting. It was the most fun I ever had running 26.2 miles.

Then there was the Year of the Feast. Bob and I had just finished our race and were heading for the car when food and drink began to materialize.

A buffet was laid out with a spread that resembled a New York Giants' training table with portions large enough to choke a python. Neanderthal-size cookies. Pasta that could feed an elementary-school class picnic. Chili in a bowl large enough to hold the Superdome—food overkill.

So we spent the next several hours sitting under the full skirt of a willow, eating and eating until Bob's wife, Susan, herded us into the van and started for home. About ten miles down the road we passed a sign advertising the world's best tamales when Bob's lunch started clearing his system, albeit not via the normal route. Susan pulled off the road and Bob ran off into the bushes.

"Are you okay?" she asked, when Bob crawled back into the van.

"It depends," he said.

"Depends on what?"

"On what you think about projectile vomiting," he replied.

After that came the Year of the Party. After the race there was music and beer—free beer!

Serbs and Croats, Israelites and Palestinians, lions and lambs will lie down together before Bob turns his nose to a free beer. So we laid back on the grass, listened to music and drank beer. Lots of beer. Then we joined the official marathon musician Ed Rinehart in a sing-along. Ed was a fixture at the Russian River Marathon. He played his multi-speakered Yamaha keyboard at every race. He knew all the Jackson Browne songs. After a few beers Bob and I thought we did, too. We clambered up to the stage and sang along with Ed, out of key, humming where we didn't know the words.

Luckily for Bob and I, at most post-marathon parties the line between acceptable and unacceptable behavior is at best hazy and at worst completely invisible. Actually, I think the other runners were delighted with this departure from protocol. To show their gratitude, they threw us in the back of Bob's van and locked us in.

There are plenty of other Russian River memories, too. Like the all-night drives to Ukiah and carbo-loading at McDonalds on Double Quarter Pounders with cheese, Fillet-O-Fish and those magical ribless McRibs sandwiches with that favorite edible mystery phrase, "meat by-products." There was the small but entirely commodious rear end of Bob's van where we slept before the race and Bob's snoring caused me many a night of colon-clenching insomnia. There was that special punishment of the Russian River Marathon—the 6:00 a.m. starting time—and there was our well-bal-

anced race morning breakfast of brownies, Mountain Dew and aspirin that
we kept in a Pez dispenser. And, of course, there was the sweet soreness of
a completed marathon.

People speak of being touched by a place or an event. I think that's true.
A race like the Russian River Marathon demands it of you. And now the
race is gone. Another marathon dies. Who will see us to the finish line now?
Who will clock us as we run into the next century? There are disappoint-
ments that may last as long as life. This is one of them.

The Miracle Race

In the interest of educating people new to the sport of running, I have prepared the following discourse on techniques employed to deal with the so-called "miracle race." If you have taken up running only recently, you may not be aware that sooner or later you will have a miracle race, a moment where all things—training, diet, rest and concentration—come together for that perfect performance. Really, it can happen.

Of course, calculating the odds against repeating a miracle race would cause a meltdown in the average computer with a Pentium chip. It is, therefore, essential that you recognize a miracle race for what it is, namely an accident resulting from nothing more than a pure and monumental stroke of luck.

Believing your own new bogus reputation can be a big mistake, because the next thing you will do is seize upon another race as if it were a juicy steak hot off the hibachi.

And fail miserably.

Slightly unnerved, you might enter a third race.

And run even slower.

Your friends will wander off chuckling to themselves, happy in the knowledge that you are not faster than they, and perhaps even a bit slower.

What happened? You made the fatal mistake of assuming that your conditioning had suddenly improved by leaps and bounds, possibly as a result of a latent speed or endurance gene suddenly kicking in, and you were overcome with a foolish sense of self-confidence. Essentially, you blew it. When you run a miracle race, your reputation as a runner is made. Don't touch it! Leave it alone!

Here's a tragic example of this phenomenon. A friend and I attended a race a few weeks back. My friend, normally about a 39-minute 10K runner, blazed to a 35-minute finish, shocking not only himself, but the remainder of the running club.

"Wow," somebody said to my friend, "what an incredible time!"

"Great race!" another person said.

Several people applauded him at the awards ceremony and the race director even came over to congratulate him.

Then I watched in horror as my friend casually announced that, in an effort to better his time, he would run the Chili Runs 10K the following weekend. I knew the look on his face well. I had seen it dozens of times before on the faces of other runners, and even myself.

Clearly, my friend hadn't recognized a miracle race for what it was. I tried to signal him by frantically shaking my head, but he was too far gone, already dreaming about hurtling through the tape at the end of the next race.

The following Sunday he ran the race and was passed at mile 5 by several senior citizens and one person pushing a baby jogger. My friend was embarrassed, of course, and I realized I had failed in my attempt to instruct him in the perils of the miracle race. He blew it because we are not talking skill and conditioning here—we are talking miracles.

This is why every runner should instantly recognize a miracle race when it happens and, if witnesses are present, respond outwardly with an expression of infinite boredom.

Witness: "Wow! I've never seen you run so fast."

Miracle runner: "Really? I thought I went out a little slow."

Witness: "Slow? Man alive, that was fantastic. What have you got planned to run next?"

Miracle runner: "Owww!"

Witness: "What's wrong?"

Miracle runner: "Gee, I think I just pulled a hamstring. That's gonna put me out of action for awhile."

With witnesses present, there simply is no way you should ever commit yourself to another race. Especially since the last one was so miraculous it practically qualifies you for sainthood (or the Olympics).

So, remember these two rules:

Rule Number One: Always respond matter-of-factly to your own miracle races in front of other runners. Be cool. Don't, for example, try to get them to sign sworn legal documents that they saw you run a personal record.

Rule Number Two: Never commit yourself to a second race. You are allotted only one in a lifetime.

My miracle race came a few years back at the Flat and Fast 10 miler.

"Cripes," said another runner. "Great race. You were really flying today."

"Do you think so?" I said. "That's strange. I felt like I was holding something back...Ouch."

"What's wrong?"

"Darn, I think my knee just went out."

I may not be much of a runner but, if I do say so myself, I'm a total master of the miracle race.

Race Day Memories

You'll have to excuse my punctuation and the depth of my vocabulary, because I'm only two years old. I'm writing this for my Pop who's busy training for his next race. He thinks that by now I should be able to evoke the day-to-day quality of life in a runner's house. It's true. I see about everything that goes on around here. What I don't notice you could fit inside the ammo belt of one of my G.I. Joe action figures. For instance, I know that when Pop's getting ready to run a marathon, he isn't exactly a model of sanity and reason.

Take last Sunday for example.

I was sitting on the toidy, chewing on a piece of zwieback, and listening to the morning noises. Mommie was banging around in the kitchen, fixing breakfast. Pop was thumping around in the bedroom, looking for his running shoes. His special ones. The shoes that he only wears on race days.

"Where in blazes are they?" he shouted. "They couldn't have just sprouted legs and walked off!"

I knew where they were, but I couldn't tell. It was a surprise. I had put them in the clothes dryer the night before so they would be all warm and comfy when he put them on. I like to do nice things for my Pop, especially when he's tapering for a race. He always gets cranky when he has to cut back on his mileage.

Unfortunately, Mommie called us to breakfast before the shoes were found. Pop came to the table in his running clothes, and boy, did he look funny! He was wearing a purple T-shirt, a yellow headband and orange shorts. Mommie thought he looked funny, too. She put palm to palm, as if in prayer, and said, "Heal him, oh Lord, for he is injured in the taste buds." Before Pop could whittle a retort to a sharp point, Mommie slipped into the kitchen to get our food.

For breakfast, Mommie and I had Quaker Oats. Pop had his usual pre-race meal of low-fat yogurt (ulp), bean curd (yuck), and mushed soybeans (ble-e-ch-h). The stuff looked like lawn clippings or cow food, but he plunged into it as though it were chocolate frosting on egg beaters. Mommie calls Pop a health-food zealot and says that he eats awful food to punish himself for being hungry. She can't imagine anyone really liking bean curd. Mommie says you never hear a vegetarian eating and saying "Yum!" and "Boy!" and "That sure hit the spot!"

After we ate, Pop went back to searching for his shoes. I tottered into the living room and flicked on the Nintendo for a quick game of Super Mario Brothers. I had just made it through level three when I heard a loud shout. Pop had found the shoes! The odd thing was, though, he wasn't as happy as I thought he'd be. In fact, he looked like he wanted to cry. I mean, his chin was trembling and everything.

"Can you believe it?" he said. "One hundred dollars worth of leather, rubber and air, up in smoke!" He was right, too. I guess I had left them in the dryer just a little too long. They looked kinda droopy, like lettuce Mommie leaves in the fridge too long.

I was about to explain until I saw that tight white look across the bridge of Pop's nose, the look he gets when he's really mad, and I decided to just hang my head and scuff some shag off the carpet with the toe of my shoe.

"I'll be right back," Pop said, throwing on his coat and rushing out the door. I knew where he was going. He was heading downtown to buy another pair of running shoes. Mommie ran outside to remind him that the only place open on Sunday was the Runner's Palace, a shoe store where the owner quoted kingly prices.

Pop didn't take the news well. He stood there for a moment, coining some colorful phrases, and then he hopped in the car. As he pulled out of the driveway I waved at him from the big picture window. He threw me a black look, but I didn't take it personally. I never do on race day.

Later, on the way to the marathon, I got my finger caught in the automatic window and my ear-splitting wail was loud enough to cause Pop to almost run off the road and into a ditch. A few miles further down the road, Pop remembered something he had forgotten.

"Did you bring my race number?" he said. Mommie looked uneasy, like all messengers with bad news.

"No," she said. "Did you?"

Pop concealed his disappointment by the ruse of pounding the steering wheel. Then he said, "I'll be a bleeping bleep-of-a-bleep," a phrase he usually only utters when our next-door neighbor's dog, Fifi, catches his calf muscle by surprise—and in violation of sense and law, did a bootleggers 180 degree turn right in the middle of the road. Let me tell you, it was keen!

Well, we made it home without injury, picked up the race number, and headed out again. Just when things were starting to get better, the car stalled. Pop lifted the hood to see what he could do, and, of course, he could do nothing. I can still see him now, staring at the engine and scratching his head, which was emitting visible question marks that looked exactly like the ones Garfield makes in the comic strip.

"Maybe we should call AAA," Mommie suggested.

"Why bother?" Pop said, pulling out a rusty screwdriver and a pair of all-purpose vise grips. "The marathon starts in an half hour. Rearranging deck chairs on the *Titanic*, that's all we'd be doing."

"I think we should call AAA," said Mommie.

"Don't bother," said Pop. "I can fix it faster myself."

It was a shame, all right. A real shame. Pop stood there for long minutes, tweaking this and screwing that, and kicking the tires. Finally he slammed the hood shut, and said, "We'd better call AAA."

A few minutes later, a big heavy man with grease all over his hands came and fixed the car real quick. It was out of gas. When we got back on the road, Pop really put the pedal to the metal. Then he looked at his watch.

"To heck with it!" he shouted, slowing down to a safe and sane 75 miles an hour. "We're already five minutes late. I give up!"

Well! There was a gasp from my nearly toothless mouth. This was unheard of. Whatever my Pop was, he wasn't a quitter. Quitting was...well, you just didn't quit, that's all. I guess Pop must have seen the look on my face, because he suddenly blushed and said, "Awww, I was only kidding."

Then he gave Mommie and me a warm, loving grin and said, "Hey, I bet we can still make it if we hurry!" And hurry we did. We sped to the race site with Mommie clutching fistfuls of dashboard, going as fast as the car and the highway patrol would permit.

Anyway, the race started late, so I'm happy to report that we made it in time. Pop got to run and everything worked out neat-o, just like it does on the Simpsons. We even stopped for pizza on the way home. Pop really surprised us by going off of his health-food diet and eating a whole pepperoni pizza by himself...but I'm not supposed to tell you about that.

And I'm not supposed to tell you about the big glass of Pepsi he drank, either. So I won't.

Pizza and Pepsi. Jeepers criminy! If you saw a character flaw of that magnitude suddenly revealed in your Pop, would you want to spread it around?

A Marathon Mantra

This is the marathon. Feel it. Breathe it. Channel its voices. Course tough? Not sure. Hilly? Dunno. Splits? Every few miles, I think. Shootin' for a fast time? Not with my hamstring. Injured, huh? Yep, I'll be lucky to finish. Same here...I'll be lucky to survive! Word of caution: Go out easy, kick in the last half. What kick? I'm just here for the T-shirt. How much time we got? Where can I pick up a number? Got any Vaseline? How's the line for the port-a-potties? Long...Use the bushes...Everyone does. That's the marathon mantra.

This is the marathon. Center yourself. Seek inner peace. Check out the competition. Cultivate that envy. Drink last night? A couple of beers. You? Haven't touched the stuff since, let's see, Friday. Sounds serious, lookin' to break three hours? I'm not racing. This is just a training run. Carbo load last night? Yep. Pasta, lots of pasta. Little salad. You? Fig bars. Fig bars? Yep. Got a marathon personal record on 'em. Fig bars, huh? Bring any with you? When's the race gonna' start? Let's get moving.

Anybody seen the T-shirt? Hope it's long sleeve. Hope it's 100% cotton. Whatja have for breakfast? Nothing...A little oatmeal. Little toast. Dry toast? Little butter. You? Nothing. Few eggs. Little potatoes. Short stack of pancakes. Can't keep much down.

What time is it? Let's get this race going. Piece of advice, double-knot those laces. Put something on your nipples. How's the line for the port-a-potties? Long...Use the bushes...Everyone does.

This is the marathon. Relax. Remove your warmups. Position your material vessel near the start. Not too far back. Not behind the strollers. Look at that guy, no socks! Take a peek at that dude. A Walkman. He's wearing a Walkman! Can you believe it? Takes all kinds. You bet. Dull world if we were all alike. How true. Evolutionary dead end. Wait a minute. Is that a walker in front of us? No way! 'Fraid so. We'll get left behind. Don't worry, we'll get 'em later. Run down the uninitiated like bunnies frozen in the headlights. Road kills, huh? Now you're talkin'. What time is it? Let's get moving. I'm getting cold. When's this race gonna start? I haven't got all day. How's the line for the port-a-potties? Long...Use the bushes...Everyone does.

This has been your marathon mantra. Memorize. Repeat. Line up according to pace.

"M" Day

Speed work. Sore legs. Hill training. Long tapers. Bad directions. No spare. Expo ripoffs. Overpriced food. Cold pasta. Noisy motels. Lumpy beds. Sleepless nights. Early wake-ups. Lost numbers. Cold coffee. Gritty Vaseline. Freezing mornings. Closed streets. Traffic jams. Late registration. Smelly port-a-potties. Crowded starts. Bossy cops. Bragging friends. Nagging doubts. Lame excuses. Smoking spectators. Race bandits. Paid rabbits. Slow pace. Deep potholes. Angry motorists. Ripped shorts. Weak electrolytes. Warm water. Hot pavement. Frayed laces. Sweaty bodies. Ugly competitors. Sunstroke. Stomach cramps. Ravaged aid tables. Inaccurate splits. Grumpy volunteers. Blistered feet. Chaffed nipples. Mental breakdowns. THE WALL. Medical emergencies. Sore quads. Walking wounded. Raw armpits. Survival shuffle. Uphill finishes. Intense fatigue. Kodak sprinters. Hamstring pulls. DNFs. Sag wagons. Bruised egos. Cruel shoes. Short courses. Clueless relatives. Bored spouses. Bloody feet. Heel spurs. Black toenails. Technicolor yawns. Missing sweats. Lousy T-shirts. Cheesy awards. Late results.

And one perfect day of marathoning to make it all worthwhile.

How Far Is A Marathon?
And other silly questions marathoners get asked most often, along with the answers.

How far is a marathon?

If the question is asked by a non-runner, the answer is 26.2 miles. If the same question is asked by the person standing next to me on the starting line at the Verrazano-Narrows Bridge, the answer is: Probably farther than you want to go today.

I can't even run around the block. How can you run that far?

A strange thing happens when a person becomes a runner. That person changes. It's kind of like watching the same species of plant mutate as you go through altitude or climate variations, a natural, predictable, yet freakish occurrence. The runner starts out by jogging a mile. A month or so later she might progress to five miles. After that, maybe 10 miles. Then 15 miles, and so forth. But a runner is never truly satisfied until she has run 26.2 miles. Why? Because runners are always in process, always trying to reach higher. For a runner, the marathon is a test of normalcy. The normal person strives for the ideal self.

Why would you want to run that far?

It is the thing that makes us pump a schoolyard swing so it goes higher and higher until we get that ultimate swoop through bottom dead center, just before the chains start to chink and fall back on themselves. It's the same urge that makes us stand up and forcefully pedal a bicycle downhill rather than merely coasting. Running a marathon pushes the horizon back, it narrows the distance between reality and aspiration, between what we are and what we can be.

Doesn't it hurt?

In every marathoner there lurks a mysterious transitional zone, a nebulous territory where the world of running meets the world of pain. It's the DMZ of running, a place where courage sometimes clashes with pain. But pain, like courage, is good. Without pain there is no adversity. Without adversity, no challenge. Without challenge, no improvement. No improvement, no sense of accomplishment and no deep down joy. Without pain, you might as well be playing Tiddlywinks.

Have you ever considered taking up a different sport?

Are you kidding? Marathoning is a solitary survivor of a long-gone time, when moral standards in sports were stricter, cleaner and somehow more easily kept. Marathoning is like a handmade mahogany grandfather clock, while the rest of athletics are akin to mass-produced, unreliable tin wristwatches that have to be set and reset constantly against marathoning's perfect movement. Most marathoners know they will never see any huge financial reward or Olympic glory from their sport. They know they will never win a race or set a national record. But still they run daily, rain or shine, with total devotion. In the I-Think-I-Can, I-Think-I-Can sport of marathoning there are other, far greater rewards. It might be the intangible rush of having run farther than you've ever run before, or the elusive moment in a race when everything comes together, fluid and graceful, and you are transported into something undefinable, something greater. Whatever it is, marathoning seems to offer something to each of us, and each of us usually finds far more than we seek.

Didn't some famous runner die while training for a marathon?

You must mean Jim Fixx, who died of a heart attack in 1984 at age 45, and who wrote *The Complete Book of Running*—an international bestseller. Actually, Fixx didn't die while training for a marathon, as most people believe. He passed away at a party when someone blew a lung full of cigarette smoke in his face.

Why do marathoners like to talk about running so much?

A marathoner without a running story is like a country music tune without mama, heartache or a pickup truck. After any race there is an almost compulsive need to relive it again and again, extolling its virtues just as a pitch man might sing the praises of a patent medicine or a thrilling sideshow. And with each telling, everything that occurred during a race becomes more. The uphills become steeper, the downhills more abrupt, the weather more intolerable. The race grows longer, but is completed with greater speed, in a remarkable inversion of the space/time continuum. And the more people around to hear the story, along with the inevitable metamorphosis that goes on with each new telling, the bigger it gets.

Don't you get bored running that far?

Bored? One of the things I love most about marathoning is that despite one's meticulous training program and the mounds of advice, the learning curve is filled with unpredictable grades. Not only that, marathoning allows you to think a thousand thoughts, see a thousand sights and hear a thousand sounds. You can free your soul and the poet/philosopher within. In a marathon, you run your feet right into Rapture. Bored? Who needs Timothy Leary's little helper when you have marathoning?

After you've run one marathon, why do another?

Competition. Camaraderie. And more than anything, peace of mind. For a sport that costs next to nothing, marathoning has given me a wealth of happiness. It's rare that I don't finish a marathon with an ear-to-ear grin on my face, warm fuzzy endorphins coursing through my body, and a question on my lips: "Where's the sign-up sheet for the next race?"

Aren't you a little old to be doing this?

This may sound self-obsessed, if not downright indecorous, to the sane, rational senior citizens who gracefully step aside for the stronger, younger generation, but: Hell no! Not me. Forget it, you smirking hip-hop earring-encrusted young dudes. You may now be the lithe and the quick, but I'm a seasoned marathoner. You may drop me in the first 20 miles, but I'll reel you in in the last six. Watch for me. Listen for my footsteps. I'll be the one with the satisfied smile on my face.

Did you see Oprah at your last marathon?

The skinny Oprah or the fat Oprah?

Running Bare

It's hot in Spokane, Washington. Darned hot. End-of-July, sun-beating-down, not-a-breeze-to-be-found hot. I hop in the car, crank the air conditioner to cadaver, and head north to Loon Lake for a weekend of camping and a 5K race. I'm a little nervous. This is not your standard, everyday running event. This is the Bare Buns Fun Run, a clothing-optional race on an unpaved forested road at the Kaniksu Nudist Ranch. I plan to run naked.

I'm nervous, yes, but I'm not about to chicken out. It takes a lot more than a bunch of naked people to rattle my cage. To some of my friends, however, the whole idea of entering a nude race was insanity, as unthinkable as traveling third class across Hindu India. And the reaction was uniformly the same: Eyes widened, pupils dilated. A great deal of winking and nudging occurred.

I refused to let it bother me. Personally, I find the thought of baring my privates in a public place to have incredible motivational power. A couple of minutes of letting that baby drill into my skull, and I'm ready to hit the ground running and not stop until I have a PR and my pants back.

Evidently, there are a lot of others who feel the same way. Nude running has taken off in the last few years. With the growth of nude recreation, many nudist resort owners have found that hosting a 5K nude race is an effective way to raise the profile of their clubs in their community, and introduce nudism to people who might not otherwise give it a try. Kaniksu's Bare Buns Fun Run, for example, attracts over 800 naked runners each year. Many do it for self-esteem. Others to be one with nature. A few, like myself, do it strictly for the T-shirt.

I arrive at the camp, fully clothed. A wave of uncertainty washes over me. Should I strip down right away, or wait until the race? I discover that it really doesn't matter. Susan Perkins, manager of the Kaniksu facility, signs me in and explains that most folks arrive in clothes, which they discard whenever they feel like it. I have plenty of other questions about nudism. Luckily, Susan has most of the answers.

No one has chased the nudist vision with more purity of purpose than Susan Perkins. It is her mission to undress America. It's an ambitious dream, to be sure, but Susan has been pursuing it for as long as she can remember.

"What kind of people are attracted to Kaniksu?" I ask. "And how do those with less than perfect shapes feel about baring it all in a public place?"

"The people who come here are accountants, business owners, doctors, engineers and retirees," Susan replies. "Folks from all walks of life. And your body is the least important thing anyone cares about at a nudist club. About one figure in twenty seen at a nudist park will be exemplary; the rest will look like people everywhere."

My conversation with Susan leaves me feeling better, but not yet ready to tear off my clothing and run unfettered into the surrounding wilderness. I set up my tent, open my suitcase, and discover that I have seriously over-packed. I've brought along a dozen changes of clothing. All I'll need for tomorrow's race are socks, shoes and plenty of sunscreen. After I settle in, I pull on my running gear and head out for a jog.

People are now pouring into camp. The place is alive with activity as I start up Ridge Trail, a steep climb that snakes around the perimeter of Kaniksu. My five-mile run is peaceful and without incident, interrupted only by a squirrel who stops long enough to hurl what sounds like a string of interspecies slurs in my direction: *Hey, buddy, this is a nudist facility! What are you doing with your clothes on?*

After my run, I head for the pre-race pasta dinner. Hundreds of runners are already in line. At the pasta feed I meet Andy and Dot Roy from Okanagan Falls, B.C. The Roys, avid sun worshipers with tans to prove it, believe nudism is the best thing to happen to American society since the advent of the five-day work week.

"Our personal philosophy," explains Dot, "is dress when practical, nude whenever possible."

"Then this must be like second nature to you," I reply.

"No, first nature," says Andy. "This is the way we'd like to live our lives."

"When you're a nudist it's soulful," says Dot. "It comes from deeper within you. You don't worry about anything without clothes on. And having no textile barriers gives you a reason not to have any emotional barriers. Nudism makes you verbalize your beliefs. It defines you as a person. I want to tell the whole country, 'Just get over it and get up here. Once you do, you won't want to leave.'"

Dot went on to explain that the Southwest Sunbathing Association has recently organized a "Nude Racing Series" at five nudist resorts in Texas and Oklahoma from August through October. Runners earn points based on their finishes, with awards given at the end of the series to those runners who have accumulated the most points.

"Runners tend to enter a lot of races and they're always looking for an extra something to spark their interest," says Dot. "A nude race is certainly something different."

Afterwards, there is time for one last stroll around the camp, then rest for the race the next morning. I head for my tent, impressed by the friendly atmosphere of Kaniksu, and by the way in which nudists like Andy and Dot seemed tuned to a deeper chord. But the final thought that crosses my mind before I drift off to sleep is: Will I panic tomorrow morning? Will I run screaming and gibbering back to my tent when it comes time to shed my clothes?

On race morning the sun breaks over the ridge and the temperature rises. Naked volunteers are everywhere, hanging banners, marking the course, and putting up signs. I trowel on my sixth coat of sunscreen, pull on my clothes, and tiptoe over the rows of sleeping runners, careful not to step on any outstretched limbs. (Let sleeping nudes lie, I always say.)

At breakfast I meet Toni, a Spokane-based runner and an avid naturalist. I ask her if she plans to run the race sans clothing.

"You bet," she says. "I love the feeling of running naked."

"You've done this before?" I ask.

"Dozens of times."

"And it doesn't embarrass you?"

Toni laughs. "Not at all. It's fun, and it promotes positive attitudes toward body acceptance. What's embarrassing about that?"

With 30 minutes until the race, it's time to warm up. I do a light 10-minute jog, stretch and line up with the others. By now there are 850 runners at the ranch, and most of them are stripping down. Before long, naked runners outnumber clothed runners almost four to one. In the name of journalistic integrity I peel off my clothes and join them.

My first thought is one of vulnerability. I feel like every secret I have is written all over my body. I am the embodiment of the *National Enquirer*. But a quick scan of the other runners assures me that I have not instantly become the center of attention.

A cannon booms, and several nude wheelchair athletes take off down the road. Five minutes later a second cannon sounds. The race is underway.

In the words of Bay Area Naturist, Pete Sferra, "Any psychoanalyst attempting to second-guess what personality disorder might cause someone to run naked might first want to try it themselves. No ulterior motives here. No childhood trauma. No looking for reactions from the crowd and no deep examination of the inner self. Just an overwhelming sense of freedom and exhilaration." That's what I'm feeling as I sprint down the road, wearing only SPF 30 sunscreen and a smile.

There's something to be said about running nude, and that's *"Awesome!"* It's like being a child again, or learning to ride a bike, or falling in love for the first time. Shedding your clothes is like peeling off layers of age.

The out-and-back course leads to and from camp. The first half is downhill to the turnaround. The person who gives us our one mile split time is naked. Spectators are naked. Course officials are naked. I'm starting to feel right at home.

I hit the halfway point greeted by a dozen naked water-stop volunteers. I'm amazed by the camaraderie of the other runners. Everyone waves and offers encouragement. Now, feeling an old hat at this nudity business (virtually all of my paranoia has subsided), I find myself doing things I might not otherwise do, like greeting people I pass. And I reveal things I don't usually reveal, like my body, blatantly exposed for all the world to see. I have discovered the most relaxing, stress-free race in the world. I dropped my drawers and dropped all my worries.

Heading back, I note that almost half of my textile-free competitors are female. I recall an earlier conversation with Susan on the subject of women and nudism.

"I wish I could address every woman in the country on the subject of nude recreation and how beneficial it is for their self-esteem," she said. "So many of them have husbands or boyfriends who would love to share the experience of total freedom with them, but women usually don't realize that there's a lot more in it for them than there ever will be for their men! For women, it is tremendously freeing to go to a place where there is no need to be concerned with how they look, much less what they're wearing! I like to tell women—although they usually don't believe me until they find out for themselves—that they can be more comfortable totally naked at a nudist club than in a swimsuit on a public beach, because they're in an environment where people are not judged by their appearance and body size, but by their personality and behavior."

I cross the finish line and claim my special "Nude Finisher" T-shirt. Kaniksu calls this a fun run, but there are some very serious competitors present. The first male finishes in 15:25; the first female in 20:29. Awards are given to both nude and clothed runners, with special awards going to those who run in the buff.

After the awards ceremony, the crowd begins to disperse. As I pack my gear, I think about how the Bare Buns Fun Run has altered my beliefs about nudism. My weekend at Kaniksu has helped me understand the hypocrisy of the enduring idea that there's something harmful or unhealthy about the naked body.

It's also shown me that clothed or unclothed, my 5K time is basically the same.

The event has ended. Time to head home. I hop in the car and drive naked to the main road. As I pull on my pants and T-shirt at the final gate, I actually feel sad. The thought that lingers in my mind is that future races will be nowhere as free and liberating as this one was.

Dot was right. Leaving camp is tough. Once you become comfortable with your nudity, it's darned hard to go back to clothes, especially in this heat.

Still The Champ

As a boy, the runner was taught to be humble, and so at first he was reluctant to write about his recent incredible sub-three-hour marathon, lest others feel inadequate.

But then the runner thought, aw, what the heck. And rushing to the computer, his fingers dancing across the keyboard, he composed the following chronicle of those magical 26.2 miles:

The morning dawned sunny, with temperatures ranging from the high 50s to the low 60s, which you don't care about and neither did the runner.

The runner was not there to measure atmospheric conditions. He was there to PR.

Over the first 10 miles, the runner blistered the course with his fast pace and near-perfect form.

"Lookin' good!" the spectators yelled as the runner flew by. And Lord knows he was flying.

At the half-marathon point the runner was informed that his official time was 1 hour, 25 minutes. The numbers barely registered. The runner did not wear a watch or keep track of his time, because he knew exactly what pace he was running. He had developed an internal stop watch.

The final 13 miles flew by. The runner's legs actually seemed impervious to fatigue, his lungs worked like bellows.

After completing the race (and not bothering to look at the clock), the runner was informed by his friends that he had just run a 2 hour, 58 minute marathon.

TWO HOURS, FIFTY-EIGHT MINUTES! The runner was giddy. His first time under three hours. This being only the runner's fourth marathon, a 2:58 sat very well with him indeed.

It was immediately after this that events in the runner's life took a sudden downturn.

Upon arriving home from the race, the runner found his 15-year-old son at the kitchen table.

"Who's the champ?" the runner shouted, waving his finisher's medal high in the air.

"You're the champ," the 15-year old said, exactly as he'd been taught. "I sense a significant event at the race today."

"Significant? Try magnificent. Try stupendous. I broke three hours!" the runner said. "No, check that. I didn't just break three hours! I shattered three hours!"

"Great news!" the kid agreed, quickly gathering up his sandwich and bolting to another room.

Finding himself alone, the runner examined his finisher's medal, intending to replay each brilliant mile of the race in his head.

Then the phone rang. The runner answered it. It was one of his friends.

"Didja hear the news?" asked the friend.

"What news?" said the runner.

"There was a problem with the race clock."

"A problem? What kind of problem?"

"Someone tripped over the cord and unplugged it. Our times are three minutes off."

As a boy, the runner was taught to persevere, to remain strong in the face of adversity. And so he will bounce back from this unnerving episode the way he always has, by becoming a tougher, more dedicated runner.

Because he's still the champ.

Nightmare On My Feet

Oh, wow—was it ever weird. I was running the Boston Marathon in hiking boots—you know, the kind with the thick Vibram soles and stiff leather uppers. And that wasn't the half of it. I must have staggered along for 25 miles, arms flailing, legs akimbo, warming the hearts of incompetent athletes everywhere, thinking I was actually going to make it to the finish—when, suddenly, my legs gave out. I couldn't run another step. There was no bounce, nothing—just splat.

Brother! It was worse than the time I got locked in the port-a-potty one minute before the start of the Bay to Breakers race. I beat on the door and hollered for help, but do you think one person in a crowd of over 100,000 would let me out? No way!

What am I still doing awake? In a few hours, I have to get up for a race. Sure, I'd like to do well tomorrow. Who wouldn't? But there's a nagging little pain in my left leg, and I'm not sure I've been training as much as I need to, and besides, I think my cold is coming back. Anyway, with the way my luck's been going I'll probably slip on my shoes tomorrow morning and there will be something horrible inside—a Gila monster or a black widow. It will bite me, and I'll drop into a month-long coma and miss the race.

And luck—you want to talk about luck? I've got the kind of luck a rattlesnake wouldn't strike at. My boss has been laying some very disapproving looks on me lately. He thinks all my dogs aren't attached to one leash. According to him, running is all I ever talk about. He refuses to recognize it as a sport, probably because you can't put other people in the hospital by doing it. With a little patience and ingenuity (and some basic information) I keep hoping that someday he'll find a little happiness outside the National Football League.

Come on, what have I got to worry about? Everything will be fine.

Then why am I still awake? A lifetime of anxiety, that's why. I remember lying awake as a kid and worrying about the next day's P.E. class where the coach would make me do 20 chin-ups, 50 sit-ups and run a mile on the track. Then I'd head back to the locker room and throw up. Things haven't changed much.

A bad case of "runner's angst," that's what I've got; or maybe it's just a stomach ache. Yeah, that's what it is. It must have been last night's dinner at one of the countless commercial institutions intent upon the "pizzafication" of our planet. Too much carbohydrate in my diet, I'll bet. Or too much protein or too much fat. Didn't I just read somewhere that a low-carbohydrate, high-fat, high-protein diet reduces endurance by as much as 50 percent? Or was it the other way around?

Maybe I'm not cut out for this. Whenever I race, I want to go faster and farther. I'm always poised at some physical crossroads with a big "S" on my chest—a future Olympic gold medalist hell bent on immortality.

So I add another five miles to my workout. I've turned my body into a human Veg-O-Matic by sprinting, stretching, chopping, slicing and grinding myself into a tortured mass of muscle. And I love it. I must, because whenever I miss a workout, guilt works me over like a professional rubber-hose man. I put my kids to sleep at night by describing the importance of economy of motion in long-distance running—my version of a bedtime story, I suppose.

What if the Chevy won't start in the morning? Or what if it breaks down on the way to the race? It's been in the shop three times and it's not even a year old. Sheeesh! If that car is "The Heartbeat Of America" it needs a pacemaker.

I've got to relax. All this worrying serves the same purpose as those braided twig-whips used by religious people in the Middle Ages to flagellate themselves. How's that song go? "Don't worry, be happy?" The man's got a point. But it's hard to be happy when you're edging toward a state of terminal freak-out.

Look at that, it's 3:00 a.m. and I'm still awake!

Did the weather report say there was a 40 percent chance of rain? I don't run well in the rain. I hope it's sunny. But then, I don't run well in the heat either. Last week, I had to cut my run short because it was too hot.

Or was that the day I couldn't dream up a decent fantasy? How did it go? Oh, right. Rob DeCastella challenged me to a race, the whole of it to be televised worldwide. The sports pages were filled with controversy: Could a relatively unknown runner defeat a world-class marathoner? There was much doubt, to be sure, but...good grief! I like to fiddle with reality when I run, but *that*—now, *that* was the dumbest fantasy I've ever come up with. I'd better watch myself, or I'll wind up in Sunnyvale Acres Insane Asylum— "basket weaving is our speciality"—sitting in a rocking chair all day, happily chatting with ghosts while a smiling nurse wipes drool from my chin.

I wonder if I'll remember to double-knot my shoelaces in the morning?

And set the timer on my watch? Did I already fill out an entry form?

Look, none of this stuff really matters. The world could end tomorrow. Gad, what a horrible thought—not tomorrow; not even next week. There's a half marathon coming up that I'd really like to run, and then I need to get in shape for—*yawn.*

Did I take my vitamins?

Did I set the alarm clock?

I wonder what I should have for breakfast? Ack!

It's like Rosanne Rosanne-dana used to say, "I'll tell you, if it's not one thing, it's another."

Zzzzzzzzzzzz.

It's Okay To DNF—Really!

The oddest thoughts flash through your mind when you're about to drop out of a race. Take my thoughts, for instance. I had just limped through 12 miles of the Napa Valley Marathon and I was completely out of steam. My legs were pumped full of lactic acid, my feet were moving at about the speed of Dutch Elm disease, and all I could think was: Find a place to stop where no one will see you.

Yes, I was hurting badly and, I shall not delude myself, filled with burning-cheek humility. One minute I was floating along on a strange three-ounces-of-gin exhilaration, soaking up the fine Napa Valley scenery, and the next, I was overcome with the sort of plummeting despair you feel when you're driving coast to coast and suddenly realize, in an isolated area, that you've been going in the wrong direction for the past three hours, the oil light is flashing and you're out of gas.

I dragged my tired, depleted, misery-ridden, and all-sorts-of-other-undesirable-things, body to the side of the road and stopped.

Did I mention that I was just a tad grumpy, too? Yes, indeed, grumpy and severely embarrassed. Since marathoners typically utter "uncle" about as often as Jackie Chan, dropping out of a race can have that effect on you.

Instinctively, I began thumbing through my Rolodex of plausible excuses: A sore knee? A hamstring pull? Heel spurs? Food poisoning? El Niño?

But the real problem, of course, was me.

I hadn't trained for the race. And let's face it, training for a marathon, like gravity, taxes and Walt Disney's hand in your pocket, is simply fundamental.

Standing there, head lowered in shame, I tried to ignore the fact that about 100 people a second were flying past me. But there was no ignoring it. Well-meaning marathoners were on me like eczema.

"Hey, that guy's dropping out," shouted one runner.

Yeah, flaunt it in genuine-in-your-face-Mister-Failure style, why don'tcha?

"Get back in here," said another.

The man deserved to be eaten by hyenas, but I'd left mine at home.

"Don't quit now," yelled a third runner.

I cringed. Whatever milliliters of confidence I had built up as a runner over the past 15 years had just leaked out of my Reeboks.

So, no, I was not in the best of humor. But sometimes, when you least expect it, fate takes a detour. Just as I began slinking, tail between my legs, toward a side road, I was rescued by two beautiful women.

Jill Hanson and Ann McKenzie, from Victoria, British Columbia, were tracking their husbands along the course when they spotted me hobbling along.

"Looks like you could use a lift," said Jill.

"Thanks," I said, climbing into the back seat of their car.

"Bad race?" asked Ann.

"Knee problems," I lied, feeling lower than ever.

Oh well, I thought. A quick trip to the motel, a shower and I could put this whole ugly thing behind me. Or so I thought.

"I hope you don't mind a few stops," said Jill. "This isn't the express run. It's the milk run."

She wasn't kidding. Jill and Ann's husbands (Bruce and George) were on a four-and-a-half-hour pace. Consequently, there was a lot of stopping. A lot of waiting. Jill and Ann made at least a dozen stops to cheer on their husbands and hand out drinks at aid stations along the way. And each time they stopped, I cowered down in the back seat to avoid being seen.

I was so angst-ridden, I needed someone to throw me a dog biscuit.

But from my hiding place, I could hear the commotion: "Come on, runners!...You guys make it look easy!...You're awesome!...Great job!"

After awhile, I found myself sitting up and taking in the proceedings.

"Lookin' good!...Go marathoners!...Keep going!"

All along the course people were handing out bananas and orange slices. A police car streamed by, booming praise.

Keep it up!...Way to go!...You're inspirational!

At one stop I watched a father snatch up his 2-year-old son, place him on his shoulders and say, "Look! There goes mama!"

I think my heart cracked ever so slightly.

Jill and Ann stuck to it, right up to the last mile. "You're almost there!...Only one mile!...You can do it!"

I must be something of an emotional chameleon, because by the time we arrived at the finish my mood had gone from crawl space to penthouse. Somewhere along the course I had discovered a few important things about running, and about myself.

I discovered that running is a catalyst for bringing good people together and forming long-lasting friendships that probably would not be made otherwise.

I found that life is truly a balancing act. In one hand, you hold your running, and in the other, you hold a job, family and other challenges that you face on a daily basis. When running is important in your life, you have to find that balance.

But, most importantly, I learned that losing or DNFing isn't really all that bad...As long as you don't make a habit of it.

The marathon will always be out there, waiting for me to return. When that happens, and rest assured it will happen, I'll be ready to meet it head on.

ANOTHER BACKSIDE IN TRACTION

Thoughts on running injuries

The Injured Runner

I just received my first injury of the season. It happened in the hills behind my home. Somehow I managed to hurt my back when I stumbled on a tree root. It could have been avoided if I'd just been watching where I was running, but you know how that goes.

At first I thought it was nothing serious, a minor irritation at best. But the next morning I could barely get out of bed. My back was killing me. So I went to the doctor and sat on the examination table, elbows on my knees, head down. I was a wrecked man with nothing to do but study my hands while some doctor made up his mind about my life.

The diagnosis was a pulled latissimus dorsi. The prescription was lots of rest. And no running for two weeks. Two weeks! My shoulders trembled, then heaved with silent sobs. God, I'm the biggest idiot in the world, I hate myself, I'm not fit to live, I don't deserve to be on this planet, I should be fired from my job, I should be starving instead of those people in India.

Oh sure, chances are I'll live. But in the meantime, while my back is healing, I'll be developing an ulcer the size of a kickball.

Being injured is no couch of roses. Having to suddenly go cold Nikes when you'd rather be pounding the pavement feels at first like being shoved out of a moving vehicle. You hit the ground hard and the car speeds away, taking with it most of your conditioning and all of your sanity. And worst of all, no one even notices that you're gone. At the most someone feels a breeze and pulls the door shut.

When you're injured, you sit and wait. And wait some more. Sometimes you walk out and get the paper. Or maybe take a nap. Or call your friends, thinking they can be counted on to sense your longing for human contact. But when you're injured friends avoid you like the plague. No one comes around to swap running stories. No one stops by to chat. You count the seconds, the minutes, the hours. Each day stretches out like a long gray corridor until you're so uptight you feel like an unflung grenade. Being felled by a vicious injury is horrible news...

Or is it?

According to a recent survey done by the Association Of Injured Runners (AOIR), the feeling of despair that accompanies a running injury is a largely under-appreciated state of mind. A natural force, it should not be chased away, but welcomed, like a summer rain. If you're injured and having a sinking spell, don't try to get over it. Get into it!

A serious funk should take the whole week. Or month. Or however long the injury lasts. A good bout of depression should make you feel almost righteous. Like you deserve a slice of pie. Like you've earned a beer and some rest. Here are a few things the AOIR recommends to help you enjoy your period of self-loathing:

Eat what you want: Forget about your runner's diet of skimmed milk, wheat germ, and non-fat cottage cheese. Adopt a new devil-may-care attitude toward food. Eat slabs of fat, mucousy casseroles and fried chicken that spurts grease until you look like you're pregnant with Baby Shamu. Oversalt your food. Become a $C_{12}H_{22}O_{11}$ (sugar) junkie. And don't forget to snack between meals. This is the way of the unhealthy. Bon appétit!

Watch plenty of TV: The average person watches six hours of television a day. That's a big block of time. But since you're no longer running, time is the one thing you've got plenty of. Sign up for cable television. Tune in to the shopping channel. Watch movies until your face has that stunned, undone look you get from being in a dark room with Sylvester Stallone. Discover exciting new things, such as why Oprah got fat, then skinny, then fat again. Overdose on TV until you're unresponsive and cyanotic. Go ahead, you've earned it.

Take up another sport: How about bowling? Or baseball? Or that game that requires you to wear a Bing Crosby cardigan and pants the color of Astro-Turf decorated with flying ducks while you stroll zombie-eyed toward a small flag rising from a well-kept lawn? Don't worry, there are plenty of other sports an injured runner can take up. And here's the favorite— bungee cord jumping...minus the cord.

Get to know your kids: Learn to mangle your syntax. Discover everything you ever wanted to know about Nintendo. Listen to their music until your skull is throbbing to the tune of the sound track of Zulu Dawn. Sit down and have a good long talk with your children. Watch them twiddle their thumbs and look as if something is biting them in a very private place.

Feed the fish. And the birds. They really need water changes. The cage needs cleaning too. Read a book. Books take up lots of time, what with all the turning pages and spelling out words. Brush your teeth, and do it with the same fierce, unrelenting ardor you used to run with. Comb what's left of your hair. Shave.

Clean your house: Spin through the apartment like a whirling dervish, finishing things you've put off for months. Scrub the Venetian blinds, defrost the freezer, wash the dishes. You've got to mow the lawn. Mulch your zucchini. Do something, anything, just don't think about running. You may not realize it yet, but after a while you'll see just how wonderful an injury can be.

Oh, and by the way, stop howling. It makes the neighbors uneasy.

The Anti-Runner

Attila the Hun was never this cruel. The Gestapo wouldn't last five minutes here. Bamboo shoots under the fingernails? Ha! Child's play. Try being an injured runner for a day. Believe me, it's a nightmare. Whether it's a pulled hamstring or a blistered toe, missing a workout can set me back the way the Sioux did Custer's hopes for Army retirement. Whenever I'm injured, I watch too much television, eat copiously and become a conduit for untold amounts of anger and frustration. To make matters worse, my friend, the anti-runner, usually comes calling.

You probably know someone like him: a know-it-all, a master of the persuasion technique called "bluntness," a one-man monument to the untested limits of cigarettes, alcohol and fatty foods, a guy who rails on constantly and with manic energy on the disadvantages of exercise, *sic* running. Why is he a friend? We go way back; we pulled pigtails together in kindergarten. And besides, deep inside his caustic exterior, he's really not that bad.

In addition to the above attributes, my friend has intuition like you wouldn't believe. He always seems to know the moment I've become injured. It must come from being such a devout anti-runner. Like a shark, he can pick up on it from miles away. When disaster strikes, he bubbles up in its wake from who knows where. Just like last month when I was out with a heel spur.

Day One:

I'm starting to lose it. I caught myself buying vowels from Vanna for intellectual stimulation when the anti-runner sauntered in, unannounced, puffing on a cigarette between bites of a triple-decker bologna sandwich. White bread, extra mayo, lots of salt. I immediately hid behind the couch.

"Hurt again, eh?" he said, pulling me out. "What is it this time?"

"Heel spur," I explained. "I'd love to talk, but right now I'm a little tired."

"Doctor said to take a few days off, huh?" he said, heading for the kitchen.

I looked at my watch. "I'd love to chat," I said, "but..."

"You're pushing your luck with all that running," he said, launching an enthusiastic search through my refrigerator. "You're living on borrowed time. Got any beer around here?"

"No beer," I confessed. "There's Gatorade on the bottom shelf."

He scoffed and strode back into the living room. "First red meat and now beer," he declared, snubbing his cigarette out on the base of my Humboldt Redwoods Marathon trophy. "You're turning into a real health nut. Running's gonna' kill you yet—"

I braced for what would come next.

"—like Jim Fixx." (The usual wearisome example.) "Or that Gabriela Anderson-Scheiss broad." The anti-runner struck a tender spot. Gabriela's performance in the women's Olympic marathon had been nothing less than heroic.

"Wait a minute," I objected, leaping up on my sore foot. "She finished the race, didn't she? How can you say that running killed her?"

"Didn't you see the way she staggered around the track?" He laughed convulsively. It was evidently one of the most mirth-provoking scenes he had ever witnessed.

"What about it?" I said. "It's called hitting the wall."

"Well, she must have hit awful hard," he laughed, going into a slapstick routine of a fatigued runner. "It left her brain-dead anyway." My temper soared to epidemic proportions.

"OUT!" I shouted. The anti-runner departed, having accomplished all that he set out to.

Day Two:

All I want is to run again. Even if it's a 30-minute-a-mile pace. On the other hand, if I can last another 10 minutes, I think I'll be able to approximate life in a coma. Between alternating fits of rage, depression and mental collapse, I made it into the second day. During an intense moment of emotional whiplash who should barge through the door but the anti-runner. "What the hell is wrong with people anyway?" he said.

"What do you mean?" I asked, adjusting the ice pack under my foot.

"Damn joggers taking over the roads. I think I hit one on the way over here." A chill traversed my spine.

"You think you hit one?" I cried. "Didn't you even stop to see if anyone was hurt?" I pictured a runner, crumpled, lying in a drainage ditch. My friend cruising by without a glance in the rearview mirror.

"Aw, I just grazed him, got any ice cream?" he said in one cerebration. Finding compassion in the anti-runner was like looking for a black cat in a dark room. I collapsed in my chair with a feeling akin to that of having mouthwash poured over a canker sore.

Day Three:
I was a total wreck. My mind was dissipating more rapidly than my conditioning. The last thing I was looking forward to was a visit from the anti-runner. Naturally, he was on me like a Krishna on an airport traveler.

"You're not looking well," he stated, in a sudden shift of concern. He knew I was weak.

"You know," I said, "my tires need rotation, and I'm late for my rolfing..."

"You look hungry. How long has it been since you had a good juicy hot dog?" Too many nitrates. But I used to love them, with mustard and catsup.

"Or a quart of Ben and Jerry's Ice Cream?" My stomach was rumbling like a herd of Zulu warriors chasing Michael Caine across the veld. I checked the window for a possible escape.

"Or a nice cold beer?" I was like Superman exposed to Kryptonite. I grew weaker and weaker.

"Gravy on your mashed potatoes? Remember how you used to heap it on?" Beads of sweat began to appear on the bridge of my nose. I tried to pick up the phone, but he had the other end of the line in his hand.

"And all those parties we used to have? Remember our parties? Up 'til 4:00 a.m. eating and boozing." He had me. My brain was turning to mush. I knew there was only one thing that was going to get me out of this. I began to feign my own death.

"Hamburgers, fries, extra grease..."
Using an Indian death mantra, I nearly stopped my pulse, but it was no use. He put a mirror to my nose to prove I was still breathing.

I was a beaten man. I knew the anti-runner wasn't going to stop until I gave in. I let loose a deep sigh and shifted my weight. My injured foot fell to the floor. No pain. I tested it again. It still didn't hurt. Again. It was fine! A wave of relief swept over me.

"Well, whatdya' say?" The anti-runner waited for my response, sensing a convert for his indolent lifestyle. "How's about you and me picking up a few six-packs and watching the ball game this afternoon?"

"Gee, I'd like to join you," I replied, slipping on my shoes and heading for the door, "but I've got too much catching up to do."

Knowing When To Quit

In my junior year of high school, at the age of 16, I dropped out of a race because of a side stitch. Immediately my coach came running over, shouting at the top of his lungs, "Why did you stop?"

"I had a stitch," I told him.

"A *stitch?*" he cried, exasperated. "You dropped out because of a little stitch? You're a quitter. There's no room on this team for quitters."

I was shocked and embarrassed at my coach's reaction, but I also understood that I deserved to be chewed out. After all, I had let the team down. I had failed to finish my race.

It is drummed into our minds from an early age that there are some things an athlete does not do. Quitting is one of those things. We are taught this lesson and are expected to abide by it. To help us remember there are numerous stick-to-the-roof-of your-skull oaths and vows of loyalty—winners never quit, and quitters never win. When the going gets tough, the tough get going. It's not over until it's over. Always go down swinging. All of these sayings add up to a single philosophy: Never let anything or anyone stand in the way of doing what you set out to do.

To a runner, such ardent dedication makes good sense. Runners who are easily turned back by obstacles may decide that the competition is too tough. Or if they do compete, they may refuse to challenge other runners or race at their full potential. In short, they may never gain a goal worth reaching.

On the other hand, there is a danger in this never-say-die school of thought. The emphasis on not being a quitter may prevent an athlete from understanding that running has stages, and that learning perseverance is just step one.

So it was with me. For a number of years following that high school track meet, I felt secure in my running, mostly because I refused to drop out of another race. At first, of course, I was only trying to prove something, but later I was trying to be something—a winner. The determination never to quit allowed me to accomplish things and run distances I never imagined possible. My 10K times came down. I ran a marathon PR of 2:43. I learned in those years to be confident, not in terms of what I had accomplished, but in what I had *yet* to accomplish, which is probably what my high school coach wanted in the first place.

While those were exciting running years, they were sometimes less than pleasant. I had more than my share of injuries. Most of my injuries were preventable, had I only stopped running or cut back when my body told me to. During one marathon I became dehydrated and passed out at the 25-mile mark simply because I was too headstrong to allow myself to quit. I measured my resolve to be a champion by how many miles I could run in a week.

Then, during one particularly tough 10-mile race, I felt something pull in my right hamstring. I came to a painful stop at the side of the road and watched the competition stream by. I was demoralized. It was the first run I had dropped out of in 20 years. Days later the pain in my leg persisted. I went to a doctor. The diagnosis: a slight tear in my hamstring. The doctor told me I had done the correct thing by pulling out of the race. Had I continued on, the damage to my hamstring could have been irreparable.

It is many years later. I have not become a quitter (giving up is not a viable way of life), but I have realized that there are times when quitting—not winning—is the right thing to do. I have learned when to stop running, when to walk away from a race, and how to accept my defeat. The lessons have not come easy, but then, good things seldom do. Just ask my high school coach.

RUNNING THE
YELLOWBRICK ROAD

Reminiscences on the beauty of running

Giving Thanks

You know what makes me sad? I mean, *really* sad? It's when runners take for granted the good things they have and aren't sufficiently thankful for what God has given them. Hey gang, we've got a lot to be thankful for. That's why we have Thanksgiving, so each of us will remember to take time out to give thanks for the many pleasures running has bestowed upon us. That, and so we can get together with other runners for an ambitious meal and an evening of conversation about complex carbohydrates and resting pulse rates that's guaranteed to leave any non-runner present in a slough of despond.

At any rate, Thanksgiving is a great idea, and this year I would like to lead the runners of America in a prayer of thanks.

Thank God for creating a sport that doesn't require the passing, dribbling, shooting, punting, hitting or catching of a ball, since in all of my previous endeavors with sports whose names end in "ball" I have never shown a molecule of talent.

Perhaps equally important, I would like to give thanks for physical therapists, and while I'm at it, thank God for Icy-Hot, aspirin and orthotics because, as every runner knows, "injury" is the most awful word in the English tongue—murder doesn't hold a candle to it and hell is only a poor synonym.

Closer to home, I would like to give thanks that my next-door neighbor, an overweight, three-pack-a-day smoker who's married to a Big Screen TV, who has a subcutaneous growth on his backside, otherwise known as a Lay-Z-Boy recliner, and who slaps his hands against his thighs to manufacture hoof beats whenever I run by, has finally moved.

I'd like to thank the Almighty that I wasn't running marathons back in the 5th century B.C., when proper running attire consisted of leather sandals, a smile and little more. Ouch!

More personally, I would like to thank the Lord that my wife is finally done flirting with her unique brand of vegetarianism, and that I will never again be subjected to another helping of yeast slurry, Brussels sprouts surprise or kelp quiche.

I must give thanks that I am finally able to afford my own motel room during out-of-town races, and that I no longer have to double up with friends who either party all night or snore so loud it's like a newsreel soundtrack of the siege of Stalingrad.

Thank God that my wife and I no longer patronize expensive French restaurants where portions are minuscule and, even after consuming everything on the menu, I still find myself rooting about the bread basket like a starving weevil.

Thank God I've finally mastered the art of losing a race gracefully, especially to women who resemble Rebecca of Sunnybrook farm, and to small balding men who look like they might be pushing 80, because it happens a lot.

And thank God for age groups, because without them my chances of victory are about as good as the chances of my kid cleaning her room without being asked.

Thank God I've learned to pick out the grains of truth from the chaff of lies, excuses and wish-it-had-of-beens whenever a fellow runner tells me about his latest race.

Thank God I'm not like my friend, who just won a three-week, all-expenses paid cruise to Hawaii on a 20-foot sailboat but has not missed a day of running in 18 years.

For that matter, thank God I have a boss who allows me time to run, and who's not like my last boss, who was so cheap he would have hired the Boston Strangler if he'd have worked for minimum wage.

And last, but certainly not least, I'd like to thank God for loving rocks, houseflies, weeds and runners above all the rest of his creations...and for making so many of us.

Thank you for the birds that sing. Thank you, God, for the sport of running.

Early Run

The kitchen floor creaks like an omen in the early light. The coffee percolates as if sending a secret code. I slip on my shoes and tiptoe to the door, careful not to wake the others. I seem to have made some kind of appointment. But for what purpose? And with whom? As I step off the porch and inhale my first breath of morning air, I remember: I'm going for an early run. And I'm going alone. For good reason.

The best time to do anything is an hour before the rest of humanity shows up. This is especially true with running. For a great run you have to get up at the crack of dawn, when the world is still soft and silent, when the air is sharp in the lining of the nostrils, like ether or peppermint.

When I go for an early run, I always go alone. It's best that way. Sparrows are my Walkman. Wild rabbits and quail my only company. The solitude alone is worth getting up early for. The bank is closed. The grocery store is closed. The world of nature is open.

My early run takes me through town. Main Street is deserted. I run along in the very center of the road, in no-man's land. Suddenly, I'm the lead runner in the Boston Marathon. I'm going for the gold at the world championships.

Anyone I see early in the morning has weight and importance. I wonder about each person, about how they came to be up at that hour. A man walking his dog—why then? Pet incontinence or simple insomnia? A security guard sitting, maybe sleeping, in a parked car. Someone in a bathrobe picking up a newspaper from the lawn.

I turn off Main Street and minutes later I'm on my favorite forest path. The trees stand close together green and somnolent. The brown-needled carpet of the forest floor is quiet under my feet. Under the silence there is an orchestra of natural music playing notes no late runner will ever hear. A small rustle from the underbrush. The groan of a tree as a breeze blows across its top. The sound of my own breathing as I move easily along.

After a time, the forest opens up to a river. Here, the trail is bordered with Queen Ann's lace and milkweed pods. Dragonflies with gossamer wings skim across the water. Stunted willows hug the riverbank and cling to life with a Schopenhauerian insistence. Running beside the mossy bank, a faint splash tells me I have surprised a frog.

A mile later the trail turns right and heads up a steep ridge. It's a demanding climb, but a beautiful one. On the low side of the ridge, as soft as a sleeping cat, lies a roll of fog. On the high side, the early morning light leaps on the eastward-facing mountains. I watch it slide southward and touch the oak and madrone trees, turning them bright as a lion's hide.

Slowly, the sun slides up higher in the sky. A whistle blows far off, summoning people to their jobs. Time to head home.

I run back the way I came, past the river and down the trail, slipping in and out of the trees with the morning sun. My pace slows dramatically as I pass by a field yellow with buttercups and a barn loft sweet with hay. A formation of swallows dives into view, pivots sharply like bats, and then chases toward the brighter part of the sky. My early run is nearly over.

Back in town the streets are alive with activity. Delivery trucks are making their rounds. People are heading to work. Music blares from radios. At the schoolyard, kids are shouting and hopping about in the morning sun like a hatch of crickets.

Once again I'm like any other runner. The rest of the world has caught up to me and when that happens, I don't get any special privileges. But I don't mind. I've had my early run. And that's enough pure happiness to carry me through the rest of my day.

Blame It On The Sun

Don't tell my boss, but the other day after I called in sick, I was out running. I said I had the flu, and I did have something—maybe not the flu, but some affliction as great—that prevented me from going to work that morning.

I think it was caused by the sun.

It's been a long, harsh winter around here. Terminally overcast. Rumpled and dreary, like Edgar Allen Poe's pajamas. This may seem a colorless little problem, when heaped next to the world's great angsts, but believe me, a steady diet of rain and fog can infest your days, your hours, your minutes on earth. Cloudy skies can turn you into a moron, a whimpering lumpish substance with a bit of spittle oozing from one corner of your mouth.

That's why whenever the clouds break, and the sun, like a winning ace up the gray coat-sleeve of winter, is played with a sudden flourish, I always seem to get sick.

Like the other day, for instance.

I remember waking up with a sun smell on my pillow and thinking, oh boy, I bet I'm coming down with something. I couldn't see the clock in all that dazzling light, let alone my car keys. In any case, the sun would hear nothing of my going to work. It pulled on my shorts and T-shirt and stuffed my feet into my running shoes.

Pretty grim, huh? It gets better. Um, ah...I mean worse.

I was almost out the door when my wife stopped me. "Where do you think you're going?" she demanded.

"I'm sick," I said. "Keep away, it might be contagious."

"Don't give me that," she said. "You're sneaking out to go running."

My wife has this thing about missing work. She insists on going in even when she's sick. Not me, though. I knew what would happen if I went to work on a sunny day. I would lapse into unconsciousness at my desk, my vital signs would stop blipping and become a steady hum, and my wife would become a weeping widow until she collected the insurance and moved to a warmer climate.

In other words, I'd croak.

Thanks, but no thanks. I'd rather stay home and suffer.

Squinting against the brightness, I was yanked out the door and into the street. Then I was pulled through town, past a little cafe, its windows steamed over from boiling coffee, through the park, and directly onto a chip-covered path.

I cannot describe my misery.

The sun propelled me on like it was a siren song and I was one of the seven seas' loneliest sailors. I was pushed down the path, past ferns, salal and huckleberry, through a grove of redwood trees as big around as FotoMats, and over fallen logs and wooden bridges.

Had enough yet? No? I'm so numb by now I can just keep on typing, but don't blame me if you just pick over your supper tonight. I was forced alongside a river flanked by gravel banks and shiny white thumbnails of sand, where steelhead trout swam lazily against the soft current and a Great Blue Heron stood waiting for a frog to make a fatal move. After that, I was thrust upon a beach, where wild strawberries, beach primrose and sand verbena clung to sand dunes.

It was horrible beyond anything the word had ever began to suggest.

By the time the sun let me run back to my house, the day was pretty much shot. And I was feeling pretty guilty. I suppose I should have spent the day sprawled beside the Sony, gorging on Hydroxes, or curled up with a *Reader's Digest* article, like, "Did Diarrhea Cause the Dinosaurs to Become Extinct?" For that matter, I could have done something *really* constructive, such as memorizing the names of all five Spice Girls. But what can I say? It was a sunny day—I *had* to run.

When you're sick, you're sick.

Why Running Can Save The World

Ladies and gentlemen, let me ask those of you up front to move back so that everyone can see and hear, for I am about to offer proof that running is the greatest sport humankind has ever stumbled upon. It can make you healthy. It can make you happy. It can make you feel like a hero. It can, in fact, save the world.

Listed below are ten reasons why running is so beneficial to life as we know it. So, if you're ready, *tah-dahhh!*

1. You feel good when you run. Running is not a hardware sport; it's an athlete's sport. The hierarchy is based on doing rather than buying or dressing or posturing. When you run, you're completely free. You're as close to nature as a wolf. You run for the same reason Thoreau sought out Walden Pond, to drive life into a corner and recapture its simplicity. Who wouldn't feel good with a sport like running?

2. It keeps you honest and humble. Running is the one oasis in life, the one area, unlike business or relationships, where one does not cheat or exaggerate. A real runner would never tell someone that they ran 26 miles if they did not. Runners also appreciate the value of winning and losing— both can carry over to anything you do in life. Didn't do so well today? That's okay. Don't worry about it. Go back, practice, come back and try again. If you do reach your goal, then victory is even sweeter.

3. It relieves stress. Running is both a private refuge and a reminder of some simpler era, a sort of crucifix thrust at the vampire of progress. No matter what's bothering you, it stops bothering you after you've laced up your running shoes. Running makes everything all right. Things begin to make original and final sense again, as they did in the beginning before you grew up and got confused. Or got half-confused, as it is proper to say of the 40-year-old boy who has resisted.

4. It works where other sports fail. Scaling a bunch of fake rocks, pedaling off into the sunset, whacking the ball around the court or logging 20 miles on the stair climber does not instill the meaning of discipline and hard work the way running does. Compared to other athletes, runners are more reserved and more intelligent, they are more dominant, more aggressive and more self-sufficient. And that's why runners have so much self-esteem.

5. It's the perfect religion. For every serious runner, there are thousands who run to hear the wind in the trees and feel the sun on their faces. For them, running is not an ordeal, but a religion. When they run, they become completely absorbed in the moment, nothing else matters and no other thoughts distract them from fully experiencing life at that instant. For a runner, the wind's mourn and whine is wiser than any psalm, prayer or profession of love. For a runner, sacredness is necessary. A runner strives to push himself, and in the process of overcoming struggles and challenges, he gets to know himself better. Isn't that what religion is all about?

6. Running only gets better when it rains. I've been pummeled by wind and rain, and I don't mind. I ran in a blizzard once that made "Dr. Zhivago" look as if it were filmed in Tahiti. I don't know why such cold gray days bring sunshine to the soul, but they do. There's something about being in the right place and doing the right thing at the right time; something about the beauty, the solitude, the adventure and the challenge of exploring new surroundings, no matter what the weather. There's something about running that makes it all worthwhile.

7. It keeps you young and healthy. Everybody's got a shtick these days, a way to help you stay young. But we deserve some integrity as we move on down the pike. Life is not a reversible commodity. Time isn't on your side. You'll find the years pass more quickly as you get older. Running improves circulation, prevents heart disease, increases the level of HDL (good) cholesterol, helps maintain weight loss, relieves stress and keeps you looking and feeling young. If only Ponce de Leon had known about running.

9. It makes for great memories. My first memory of running is with the family dog—a spastic mutt who would chase after me, knock me down and lick my face as I giggled, half-trying to push the slobbery dog away, half reveling in the torment. My favorite memory is of a race I won. There are a thousand other special memories, every one of them equally as precious. Ask any runner, they will tell you that remembering a run is almost as good as going on one.

10. There are a lot of us around. To borrow a line from every comedian in the world, I know you're out there—I can hear you breathing. I really can. I've met you on the street, chatted with you as we did laps on the track, ran behind you as you raced through the forest. I feel as though you're looking over my shoulder as I tap out this story. And I know that you'll agree with me: Running *can* save the world.

Going Sane

I think I might be going sane. I can't pinpoint with certainty the moment at which it seemed to happen, or even how. All I know is that since I became a runner, life inexplicably seems worth living again.

Nice, yes. But as a friend recently said, "If you allow yourself to become sane, think of all you'll be missing out on."

"What?" I asked him.

"For one thing, your eating habits will change," he said, gravely shaking his finger at me. "You'll be wanting less red meat and more vegetables."

"Well, I have been trying to cut down on beef," I admitted.

"Disgusting," murmured my friend. "See what running is doing to you? Red meat, 22 meals a week. Now *that's* the formula for keeping America fit."

"And I like vegetables," I said. "They're my favorite food."

"Vegetables aren't food," he replied, patting me on the shoulder with patronizing and perfunctory sympathy. "Vegetables are the stuff that food eats. People should eat *real* food, like the stuff you hit with your car in Texas."

"Look, I assure you—"

His voice came back like a fast serve. "Oh, sure, the road to sanity may be tempting, but believe me, it's paved with nails. Here's something else you'll be missing out on—you'll be so busy running, you won't even have time to watch TV."

Oh, yes, the nightly worship of the tube. People glued to their color sets, sitting through the pap of sit-coms and game shows and private detective movies with their jaws open and their minds closed. "Well, I have been turning in earlier," I said.

Distaste was written all over his face in a dozen tight places. "Look, in spite of every logical instinct I've ever had, I still consider you a friend, but this is definitely getting out of hand. All this running, holding down cholesterol, getting plenty of rest—why put yourself through such misery?"

"*Misery?*" I said. "That's one of the most common misconceptions people have about running. It's not difficult, it's downright enjoyable! Since I started running, I've been more relaxed—no more tension or anxiety. And running is a sport everyone can enjoy. It doesn't take a lot of expensive gear. It doesn't even take any special talent. I like everything about running. I even like the competition."

"Wait a minute. Whoa, *whoa*. Run that by me again, please?"

"You mean about how relaxed I've become?"

"No, no—the part about the competition." He grinned, but with little or no humor. "So, you like racing, do you?"

"I love it."

"And tell me," he said, with all the incredible delicacy of arthritis, "have you ever once *won* a race, or even come close?"

Ooh. A low blow. I wasn't sure how to answer. No, I'd never won a race. And with times like mine, I probably wasn't ever going to win anything, but ah, the fantasies! "Well, not really," I said, "but—"

Again, his taut, measured replica of a smile. "Ah-ha, the mystery deepens!" I wanted to escape, but judging from the look of determination on my friend's face, it would be a three-crowbar job to pry myself away.

He blundered on: "You know what your problem is? You're looking through the wrong end of memory's telescope. Remember slaking your thirst with a six-pack of Budweiser between bites of a triple-decker bologna sandwich, white bread, extra mayo, lots of salt? Remember partying until 2:00 a.m. and sleeping until noon? Remember the taste of a cigarette after a good meal?"

"I think I must have forgotten," I said.

He expelled air through his lips the way you do when you're at wits end. "A punishment is needed for people like you," he said. "You should be strapped down in front of a big screen TV for a full month and forced to watch nothing but game shows. You should be locked in a closet and left there until you've developed an insatiable appetite for bacon, whiskey and mayonnaise."

"I'm sorry," I said, not really feeling very sorry, "but going sane just doesn't seem that bad to me."

"Can't you see that you're not functioning as a responsible citizen?" he said, howling out truth and patriotism the way a seal bites out the National Anthem on a row of circus horns. "What would this country be like if everyone took up running? Think about the unemployed tobacco farmers, bartenders and heart surgeons. Think about the unemployed psychiatrists. Why, it's un-American not to be in therapy! Is going sane *bad?* Hah! Is the pope Catholic? Is John Cougar Melencamp from a small town? Of course it's bad. It can ruin our economy, shut down our pharmacies, lay waste to every fast food franchise in the country."

"I had no idea that I was such a menace to society," I said.

He moaned unhappily. "Hear that moan? That's the cry of an outraged American demanding that you be forced to act like the rest of us."

"You mean like driving two blocks to the store instead of walking?" I asked.

"Exactly," he said.

"And eating fried food at least three times a day?"

"That's the ticket."

"And watching sports instead of participating in them?"

"Now you're getting the picture."

"Well, I'm sorry," I said, "but that's no longer the kind of lifestyle for me."

"Oh, I forgot," he said, with the sneer of the smug Puritan pitying the sinner condemned to eternal torment, "you're turning into a real crackpot, aren't you?"

I smiled. A crackpot? Maybe, maybe not. It really didn't matter. I suppose nothing much does when you're going sane.

Beyond The Comfort Zone

It's Monday morning and I'm just back from the Road Runners Club of America (RRCA) National Convention. My notebook should be a gold mine of crisp facts, fond memories and vivid impressions, but reality is a few pages of nervous scrawl punctuated by references cryptic enough to puzzle even this red-eyed writer. For instance, what exactly does "The horror, the horror" mean?

Oh, yes, now I remember: the RRCA Awards Banquet, and my speech. Now there was a frightening evening. One that ranks just behind divorce and nuclear war as cause for sheer terror.

But distance lends perspective, they say, and by now the epic misery has, in a strange way, mellowed into an amusing story and a kind of permanent brain damage. Allow me to sift through the frayed details of my adventure with what little mind I have left.

Imagine yourself in a nice, quiet hotel room far from home with no lawns to mow, no lunches to make, and no job to worry about. Imagine running twice a day and making pilgrimages to the far-flung corners of the Great Smoky Mountains. Imagine sleeping in late and waking to a full, uninterrupted hour of CNN News with no one leaping on your chest demanding a diaper change or a bottle of milk or screaming, "I want Disney! I want Disney! "

Imagine your face slowly freezing into a smile of indescribable bliss.

Such was life (for four days, anyway) at RRCA's 39th annual convention in Knoxville, Tennessee. The convention, hosted by the Knoxville Track Club (KTC), featured workshops on race directing, computerized timing, kids' running programs, the Internet, women's safety, race sponsorship, newsletters, course measurement and a highly entertaining talk on adventure running by *Runner's World*'s Bart Yasso.

There were receptions, parties, morning fun runs and sight-seeing trips through Knoxville's Old Town. There was the RRCA National Championship News-Sentinel EXPO 10,000-meter run and (check this out!) a chance to rub elbows with some of America's finest distance runners.

For instance, I had a casual fellow-out-back-on-Saturday mode of conversation with Olympian Ed Eyestone, a feet-on-the-desk confab with Olympian Pete Pfitzinger, and a spirited one-on-one discussion with *Runner's World* senior writer (and new RRCA President) Don Kardong:

Me: (holding a copy of Kardong's new book *Hills, Hawgs & Ho Chi Minh* that I purchased earlier that day) Hey Don, could I get you to sign this for me?

Kardong: (eying me suspiciously) Did you pay for that book yet?

Me: (caught off guard by the implied accusation) Well, uh, you see...

Kardong: (signing the book, handing it back) Now you're sure you paid for this?

Heady stuff, huh? Who wouldn't think the horn of plenty had been laid, big end forward, just outside the door of my hotel room?

Then, on the final day of the convention, I was snapped back to my senses by a big dose of reality. As RRCA's Club Writer of the Year, I was expected to give a speech that evening at the Awards Banquet. No big deal, right? A simple five-minute speech. Then why did I feel as though I were about to enter the gang-infested waters of South Central Los Angeles?

Public speaking is a rush that, a lot of people will tell you, is higher than any race they've ever run or even heard about and maybe even better than winning the Boston Marathon. Personally, I fear speaking in public the way others might fear a crippling disease or death itself. I've always been the kind of person who flushed red up to my scalp if the focus of a group ever narrowed to me. And now I was being asked to speak in front of an audience of over 400 movers and shakers of the running world.

How I would make it through the evening was beyond me.

As I sat on my hotel bed, the air conditioning unit blowing brisk, chemically cooled breezes across my sheets, I sweated to find the proper words for my speech. But my mind was bracketed, limbo'd, unable to budge or strike a spark. A ream of crumpled papers lay about me and not one solitary thought written down.

I had waited until the last minute to prepare my speech, which is typical for me. I live in a perpetual state of fourth-and-long, always running late, grasping desperately for the slippery short end of the baton and continually battling my own lack of forethought with come-from-behind pressure cooker heroics. With less than an hour to go before the Awards Banquet, I was cookin' big time.

Outside, a sprinkler turned on the lawn, making a hisha-hisha-hisha sound as it cast rainbows in the air. An empty page stared back at me with the quiet challenge of the crossword puzzle in *The New York Times*. I wrote:

"Good evening. It's great to have so many friends in running who love the sport and the lifestyle...

"Hi. I think that runners are generally very positive people who like to make the most out of life and..."

Sheeesh! Nothing sounded good. Nothing sounded like I had even half a brain. Desperation was a knife at my back. I snatched up the phone with shaking hands and dialed Laura Kulsik's room.

Kulsik, RRCA's Western Region director, was an old hand at dealing with large crowds. For her, public speaking was as natural as grass sprouting. Maybe she could help. Kulsik answered the phone on the second ring.

"Hello-o," she said in a happy, airy voice, as if she'd just been in the yard, pinning up clothes on a sunny line.

I explained my problem as calmly as possible. "You've got to help me, Laura!" I whined into the phone. "I can't make that speech tonight. If I go up on that stage I'll slip into a tongue-thickening, brain-stalling torpor and start making Porky Pig noises (bdee, bdee, bdee...)."

To my endless gratitude, she did not laugh out loud. She knew that this speech was gnawing on my nerves like rats on a rope.

"You'll do fine," she said, "just relax."

"Relax?" I cried "You should see me speak in front of a group of people. I look like I'm making a hostage tape. I sound as though I studied elocution at the Sylvester Stallone School of English."

"All right, calm down," Kulsik said. "Let's hear what you've written so far."

"Hello runners ..."

"Hello runners? Okay, that's a start."

"So, what should I say next? I can't keep saying, 'Hello runners, Hello runners, Hello runners' all night!"

"Say whatever comes to your mind," she suggested. "Try something inspirational."

"Inspirational? Are you kidding? I couldn't inspire a frog to croak!"

"Look, all you have to do is just give it your best shot," said Laura. "What have you got to lose?"

Her facetious epigram reminded me of the rakehell quip of a soldier before battle. And yet, she was right. What did I have to lose?

"Okay, Laura," I sighed, "I'll give it a try."

I glanced at my watch. It was time to go. I had to come up with something fast, but I was too nervous to think. My mind was a total blank. I could just as well have been balanced on a spider-infested log in a sewage lagoon, that's how anxious I was.

As I pulled on my clothes and bunched up my blank notes, I thought about what Laura had said: "Just go up there and give it your best shot. What have you got to lose?" I headed downstairs and in the direction of the Awards Banquet, clinging to that thought with the ferocity of a pit bull on a pant leg.

The physical sensation of a panic attack is familiar to anyone with an unhealthy fear, or phobia, whether it's crossing bridges, stepping into enclosed rooms, flying airplanes, whatever. A feeling of anxiety washes over you in waves. You grow hot when you shouldn't be. And if you're lucky, you pass out.

I didn't pass out. But as I walked into the banquet hall, I came awful close. Stepping into that room was almost an out-of-body experience. My mind was reeling under a sensation of utter helplessness. I felt like a zombie on the way to its own beheading.

I sat down at my table and the evening's festivities soon got underway. First came dinner, during which time I sat there and clutched a glass of beer in my hand as if it were the ejection lever of a flaming jet. Then came several speeches by RRCA officials, during which time I scribbled madly, writing down last minute notes like a census taker on amphetamines. And finally, the award winners began to file up to the stage.

There was Henley Gibble (Fred Lebow Women's Running Award), Jim Duguay (Outstanding Club Volunteer), Gary Franchi (Outstanding Small Club Newsletter), Joan Pribnow (Outstanding Medium Club Newsletter), Cynci Calvin (Outstanding Large Club Newsletter), Beverly Coville (Reebok/RRCA Outstanding State Rep) and Knoxville Track Club's Michael DeLisle (winner of the '94 Club Newsletter and Club Writer Awards) and a host of other impressive people.

Before long there were only two award winners left: Tom Derderian (Journalism Excellence Award) and myself. Derderian walked up to the stage, spoke eloquently to the crowd and drew a nice round of applause...

And then there was one.

I felt myself turn white. I would have rather been anywhere else at that moment. Like, say, sponge bathing a rabid wolverine. Or standing in front of a pay toilet with diarrhea and no dime.

Then, just as I was about to fold like a Mexican road map—a miracle!

Keynote speaker (1972 Olympian) Jeff Galloway bounded up onto the stage in a blind burst of personal kilowattage to deliver his speech. It was at that moment that an idea struck me. It hit me, as Col. Kurtz would say, like a diamond bullet between the eyes.

Galloway is a kind of Winnie the Pooh in running shoes, ambling along, writing books, giving speeches and making friends wherever he goes. He is a busy man, yet despite the obvious pressure he appears calm and unruffled. With Galloway there is always time for a long, leisurely run or a friendly chat. There is always time for others. He is the sport's ultimate totem of breezy, permanently sunny Taoist fecklessness. You'd be hard pressed to find a more likable guy.

Earlier that day, while tagging behind Galloway in the 10K Championship, I watched him stop in the middle of the race and help a fallen runner off the course. One runner helping another. A simple act of kindness. Not exactly the kind of stuff that would make the evening news. But it started me to thinking about similar acts of camaraderie and compassion I had witnessed during my years as a runner.

Most runners realize that they will never see any huge financial reward or Olympic glory from their sport. They know they will never win a race or set a national record. But still they run daily, rain or shine, with total devotion. Why? Because in the sport of running there are other, far greater rewards.

It might be the intangible rush of having run farther than you've run before. Or the elusive moment in a race when everything comes together, fluid and graceful, and you are transported into something undefinable, something greater. Or maybe it's the thick, visceral camaraderie that the sport offers, the mysterious bond that unites runners and gives them a glimpse of some greater unity and purpose.

Running seems to offer something different to each of us, and each of us usually finds far more than we seek, so that in the end it becomes hard to tell one runner from another.

I thought about all this, and I began to realize what a great bunch of people runners are, no matter what they have done, no matter how fast or slow they run, no matter where they travel, like Galloway, they all have the milk of human kindness floating through their veins. So many good people. So many kind souls. All of them runners.

My name was called. Suddenly I was wide awake, brain cells flashing like free-game lights in a pinball machine. I stood up and strode to the stage like Shane unleashed, like Kid Lightning, hands wrapped, warming up for the main event. I stepped up to the microphone wearing the confident smile of the high school nerd who's done all the tough extra credit homework.

Well, maybe I wasn't quite that confident, but I was able to hold back the terror, purge the mind riot and give my humble little speech. And since I didn't see anyone rolling their eyes, or looking at me, blankly, totally without comprehension, as though I were speaking in Sanskrit or Basque, I suppose you could say that it went okay.

There's probably a moral in this story somewhere—a bottom line, a grain of truth, a kernel of knowledge. But what? Maybe you could say that public speaking is a lot like running: You must have a lot of faith in yourself and give it your all...or at least your most...or whatever you have available without making special arrangements.

TANGLED UP IN SHOES

Runners and their shoes

New Keds On The Block

George Washington crossing the Potomac!

Charles Lindburgh flying into Paris!

Me, zipping home from the Joggn' Shoppe in my brand new shoes! Which I did today, *exxxtra* carefully.

Buying a new pair of running shoes is exciting. Better than Christmas, even. It's the one time in a runner's life when he can feel dead rubber and leather come to life and suddenly sprout nerve endings directly into his feet. New running shoes have mystical powers of rejuvenation: They can turn a worn-out marathoner into a born-again sprinter. They can conjure up visions of personal bests. Course records. Olympic gold medals! There's no end to the many pleasures of new running shoes.

It even gets better when the new shoes are a pair of Asics Epirus.

To the untrained eye, the Epirus doesn't look like much—it has none of those bells-and-whistles features you find on other shoes. No velcro straps; no colors that would have made Picasso cringe; no special mutant-ninja mid-sole technology designed for the bio-mechanically damned. Nothing fancy. The Epirus is without any special gimmicks. Just an average-looking shoe that was constructed, as opposed to over constructed, to do the relatively simple job of securing a runner's foot as it repeats a motion a thousand times per mile. And it does that incredibly well. Better than any other shoe on the market.

So, wouldn't you know it, the company has stopped making them.

That's right, the beloved Asics Epirus has been terminated. Canceled. Kaput! The few pair that are left floating around have become an endangered species, kind of like the whooping crane. It'll probably be a long time before anyone comes out with a shoe like the Epirus, so for now, I'm taking excellent care of mine.

That's why, on my maiden run, I'm trying so hard to avoid puddles, potholes and dusty thoroughfares. That's the reason I'm steering away from yelping teenagers in fast cars with squealing tires, and giving a wide berth to gigantic trucks full of boiling asphalt and crews of wild-eyed men wearing hard hats and carrying picks and shovels.

It's not as easy as it seems.

My Epirus seem to have grown to the approximate beam width and keel length of the aircraft carrier *J. F. Kennedy*, and I've decompressed to a whimpering blob of protoplasm, wondering why on earth I decided to wear them home on a day like this.

The weather report said there was a 90 percent chance of rain. And the sludgy ebb and flow of small town traffic has turned kinetic, sinister, mean. Somebody has paid every insane driver in the immediate area to come after my shoes and take turns trying to dirty them up.

A bearded bandit on his Harley-Davidson motorcycle pulls up beside me, checking out my Asics. I slip around the biker and find myself face to face with a high rider—a tobacco-spitting, T-shirted cowboy driving a four-by-four road tank with chrome-plated roll bar and a bumper sticker that reads: "If You Don't Like The Way I Drive, Stay Off The Sidewalk."

My precious Epirus have about as much chance as a cat at a Doberman convention.

But in my sweaty panic I've quite forgotten that new shoes—for eight hours or eight miles, whichever comes first—dwell in a separate and superior dimension of space and time and are impervious to all dirt and grime.

I make it home without incident; my Epirus escape miraculously unscathed.

Not that relaxation follows, mind you. Not that I can let down my guard. Even as the run winds down I'm noticing, with nerves still sensitized—nay, twanging—little things I'd never noticed before. For example, the neighbor's dog, which is cutting teeth and looking for something—anything—to chew on, is nosing around our porch. And my teenage son, who has the terrible habit of losing everything he borrows, is scouring the house for some footwear to go with his acid-washed Levis. And my wife, who has been known to turn perfectly good running shoes into filthy garden clogs, is poking around in my closet.

I think I'll put my Epirus under the bed tonight for safekeeping...

I'll probably be awake half the night worrying about them. When morning comes—if it comes—and by some remote chance my shoes are still under my bed and not on the feet of some cat burglar running down Main Street, boy, am I going to take care of them. No muddy trails. No rainy-day runs. A once-a-day—no, make that a twice-a-day—wipe-down with a damp rag. My Epirus will be the most well-kept, well-maintained, non-abused running shoes anyone's ever seen.

Hold it. Wait a minute. Who am I fooling? I should know better than anyone that it's impossible to keep running shoes new forever. One day I'll get caught in an unexpected rainstorm. Soon afterward, I'll be asked to go on a trail run by friends and end up a muddy mess. Road tar and grass stains will start to defile their color. My pristine shoes will thenceforth begin their decline into ordinariness.

Rain. Mud. Road tar. Grass stains. Hmmmm. Turning my new Epirus into just another pair of old running shoes might not be such a bad idea after all. I'll be having so much fun wearing them out, I won't have time to worry about it.

If The Shoe Fits

I wasn't sure what to expect when I showed up to the workout wearing sneakers. A little good-natured ribbing, perhaps, about how cheap they looked. Or maybe a cutting remark or two about their origins. I was ready. "Sure," I'd say, "I got them at K-Mart, and"—the clincher—"they only cost $10.99."

What I wasn't prepared for was the silence. And those occasional side-long glances. Standing among my fellow runners, I felt a sudden twist of Scrooge-miserliness. I was so embarrassed by my shoes, I ran home and changed into a more appropriate brand.

We are living in shoe-proud times. Even I will admit that at first I had misgivings about buying a pair of running shoes costing roughly as much as a meal at Burger King. In this age of expensive footwear for maladjusted metatarsals, for the fleet of foot or fat of thigh, what do sneakers (even the word has become *declasse*) say about your character? The shoes look cheap, an affront alike to conspicuous consumption and modern technology. They're considered among many to be the Styrofoam of running shoes. A collector's item wherever low camp is a synonym for good taste.

So what? I think it's time someone spoke up for sneakers. They may not look it, but they have a lot more to offer than you might think. In some ways they are just like their expensive counterparts.

Sure, you say. Right. And a bicycle is "just like" a motorcycle, except it doesn't have an engine. A book is "just like" a painting except it has words. Eternity is "just like" Sunday except it's longer.

Don't get me wrong, I'm not trying to take anything away from today's state-of-the-art running shoes—Nike has its Air sole, Asics has its Gel, and Reebok has its Energy Return System. Other shoes even have built-in computers on board that tell you everything except what you'll be having for dinner.

I just think this country's going through a midsole crisis.

The modern-day sneaker is a changed shoe. It's a lot different from those clunkers you wore back in high-school gym class. Granted, they might not have full air insoles, or a Kevlar bar to eliminate torsional movement, but they do have adequate cushioning and stability. They don't have colors that leap out at you like shouts from a carnival barker, or a high-tech NASA testing-ground look, but they don't have price tags based on ballplayers' salaries either. Here's a shoe you can wear out in the pouring rain. Here's a shoe you can slosh through ankle deep mud in. And you don't even have to worry about taking out a second mortgage on the house.

Somewhere along the line, we were led to believe that expensive shoes would make us go faster, farther. Nothing could be further from the truth. Everyone should know by now that you can't buy your way to fitness, let alone a marathon PR. I have a friend who runs a 32-minute 10K. He favors JC Penny's brand sneakers, the ones with the Velcro straps. You should see the look on the competition's face when he blows by them. Shoes that talk softly by no means reflect on the size of your stick.

Now, despite the occasional sneer, I have the confidence that comes from owning sneakers. They can't count calories, of course, but stepping into them is like stepping back into childhood. Besides, I say if the shoe still "fits," wear it.

Dreaming The Dream

The man behind the shoe display was caressing a pair of racing flats. He was in love.

"Feel these," he said. "Go on, hold them in your hands. Have you ever felt a lighter pair of shoes in your life?" He shoved the shoes in my face. There was nothing to do but feel them.

It's what happens at pre-race marathon expos. You wander around and salesmen hand you shoes. "Hey, you, take a feel." There were lots of different shoes to caress at the California International Marathon pre-race expo in Sacramento, where thousands of runners came to pick up their race packets, look at running gear and size up the competition.

Getting into the expo cost nothing but nerve. It's easy to psych yourself out before a race, especially when you check out the other runners. Marathon runners resemble no one else. They're as lean as whippets, as sinewy as jaguars. They look fast.

Two runners beside me were discussing pre-race strategy.

"I'm going to take it out at a 6:25 pace," said one marathoner.

"I want to run 5:45 splits for the whole race," said the other.

I tried to remain calm. Sure, I thought, sizing them up. They can talk the talk, but can they walk the walk?

There were young marathoners and old marathoners at the expo. There were men and women marathoners. They all had one thing in mind—a fast time in tomorrow's race.

"Buy a pair of these shoes," the salesman was saying, "and I can almost guarantee you a good race." I bought the shoes. They cost $102.99, which is a lot for a pair of running shoes and a slim guarantee. Expo shoe salesmen really know how to get to you. I would have bought his entire company if he would have guaranteed me a PR.

Every shoe in the place was amazing. Every shoe could save you precious seconds. One shoe had air. Another had gel. A third had an Energy Return System (ERS) that recycled wasted energy back into your legs. The salesman shoved a pair into my face, turning them over so I could get a bird's-eye view of the wonderful ERS. I didn't mind. It was too wondrous to behold. I bought another pair of shoes for $115.99. I had to have them.

Next to the shoe displays were the energy drinks, of which there were at least 20 varieties.

"You'll never hit the wall again," said one salesman. "A cup of this before the race and you'll feel like an Olympian for the entire 26.2 miles."

A booth at the far end of the room was selling little tags that attached to your shoe identifying you in case of an emergency, but no one was buying. Pre-race expos are for dreaming the dream, for fantasizing about the perfect race.

"No one thinks they're going to bomb in a marathon," said the salesman. But then, no one wants to consider something like that the day before a race.

Tennies From Heaven

"Tiger to merge with Reebok," the headline says. That's big news. I'm guessing that the two shoe companies are evidently working on a better running shoe for several reasons:

1. To keep pace with the hot, young, active lifestyle-enhancing athletic shoe market.

2. If they don't do it, someone else will.

3. It's like life on Mars: Man will never abandon the search for the perfect running shoe.

So, Tiger and Reebok are creating a new high-tech running shoe. Ha! If you're planning on buying a pair and you hear a sound like a Phantom F-4 fighter behind you, move to the side of the road immediately. I'll be coming through in my Future Shoes.

What's a Future Shoe? Simply the most incredible, state-of-the-art running shoe ever made.

Here's my plan: Future Shoe will incorporate the finest cushioning technologies of every running shoe on the market. They'll have a Grid system, Pressurized Air, Rollbar Stability, Saddle Support, Silicone Gel, Hexalite cushioning *and* Abzorb Suspension.

Looking for something better than the Next Big Thing? Today's strutting display of foot plumage won't stand a chance against Future Shoe. Just check out these occupant amenities: Dei-Lex Lining, Steel Shank, Metatarsal Pad and a dandruff fighting foot insert.

Do your feet pronate? Do they supinate? Are you a heavy heel striker? A toe striker? Do you have high arches or flat feet? No problem. Future Shoe will cure all that and more. It will provide maximum support, traction, wearability and be compatible with Windows 2001.

How'd you like to be a champion distance runner? Future Shoe will give you the kind of respect you've earned as a marathoner, but simply don't always get. You'll set a course record at Grandma's, blaze to victory at Boston, knock 'em dead at New York.

What about the Kenyans? Ha! Don't you hate it when you're running a marathon and the people in front of you won't get out of the way?

No more of that gee-whiz-what-will-they-think-of-next stuff. Future Shoe will always be, to coin a phrase, "what's happenin'." Wear any other brand of running shoe in its presence and risk getting squashed like a small emerging Central American nation with rich oil deposits.

Future Shoe will be the finest running shoe this year.

This decade.

This century!

Race director: I'll be lining you up according to overall shoe quality today. What kind of shoes are you wearing?

Me: Future Shoe.

Crowd of bystanders: Oooooooo

Future Shoe won't just be footwear, it will be an attitude. A go-for-it kind of running shoe that will become the mantra of the next decade. No fear. No limits. No excuses.

An additional bonus: Future Shoe will cure Achilles tendinitis, plantar fasciitis, side stitches, shin splints and, possibly, diarrhea.

In keeping with our politically correct times the Future Shoe will not be sewn by 10-year-old Sri Lankans working 18 hours a day in windowless factories. These shoes will be hand-sewn with American thread by American seamsters who will be paid by American entrepreneurs who donate a percentage of every shoe to help train future Olympians throughout the world.

Did I mention that the Future Shoe will be available in over 1,000 dazzling Da-Glo colors and come with a 500,000-mile guarantee?

Oh, sure, Future Shoe will be a little pricey ($3,745, plus tax). But look at what you're getting! A shoe that's made of Adiprene, Etxlite, Polyurethane, Cambrelle and a dozen other yet-to-be invented fabrics and plastics. Remember, it's safe to take the low bid on socks and underwear, but with running shoes, let *value* be your primary concern.

A word of warning. Don't wait until Future Shoe goes on sale. Buy a pair now or they'll be tougher to find than a nesting pair of peregrine falcons.

Still not interested? Okay. Fine. Have fun in your outdated, under-engineered Precambrian running shoes. I'll see you at the finish line in my Future Shoes...if I don't fall asleep waiting for you.

Strictly Singlets

This came to me in the mall the other day as I walked past Sally's Salt Shaker Haven and Manny's House of Lead Pencils and the bench where all the battle-fatigued mothers with howling, unruly children gather to catch their breath.

A shoelace store for runners. No, I'm serious. Call it something catchy, like, oh, The Lace Place. Or maybe Knot For Everyone.

Two thousand feet of floor space is what I envision. Row after row of shoelaces, laid out under a long glass display case, everything from your basic white cotton laces to the more flashy Day-Glo colors.

Think about the trouble you go through now to buy a new pair of shoelaces.

Maybe you shop at one of those large chain stores where they make you wade through racks of shirts and shorts while an officious looking man in a referee's uniform tries to talk you into a pair of $150 computerized, state-of-the-art basketball shoes. When all you wanted was shoelaces.

Or you go shopping at a discount store like K-Mart, where you get squeezed in a Blue Light Special on Charmin toilet tissue.

The point is, the age of specialization is here. Focus on one item and one item only. That's the name of the game. Everyone's doing it, why should running be left out? Really, this could have *far-reaching implications*. Hey, I hear a certain famous ex-marathoner—no names, please—is thinking about opening up a whole line of sweatband boutiques.

Maybe only *wrist* sweatbands, too. Can you imagine?

Anyway, the other idea I had is Strictly Singlets, which would be pretty much what the name implies.

Finally, you'd have a running store devoted entirely to singlets. We would carry every brand of singlet imaginable. And every size too—infant to XXX-large. There would be a bulletin board by the door crammed with news about the latest in singlet technology.

Someone comes in looking for a pair of shorts, you show them the door.

"You want The Short Stop," you say, politely but firmly. "Second level, side, next to Heather's Hot Plates."

Pretty soon, each time the little buzzer beside the door goes off, you'd know it's not someone looking for Gore-Tex gloves or Bill Rodgers warmups or a fanny pack for their Walkman.

I'll tell you something else I'd like to see—a store that just sells body fuel replacement drinks like ERG and Cytomax and Gatorade. There are a lot of thirsty runners out there and we're not doing enough to help them.

Anyway, you go with a rehydration theme here and call the store something like, oh, Glucose 'R' Us. No, maybe that's too flip. How about Sports Drink Chalet? No, too...I don't know, European.

Wait a minute! Bill's Body Fluid Palace. There you go.

Now, unlike Strictly Singlets, we'd want to expand the focus a little and treat a broad range of thirst problems: total dehydration; fluid replacement; intercellular deficiency—that kind of stuff.

At least for the first few months, advertising would be an imperative. You'd want a lot of signs in the front window geared to mall traffic, such as:

"Gookin-Aid Prepared While U Wait!"

"You Won't Go Away Depleted!"

"Electrolytes Replaced Or Your Money Back!"

Look, the place would be nothing fancy. We'd go with the standard running store furniture and five-year-old issues of *Runner's World* magazine lying around. And maybe we could pipe in some relentlessly cheerful elevator muzak. The totally dehydrated are said to find such melodies soothing.

And get this: For those customers who demand privacy, at the rear of the store we will have private drinking booths.

Is that neat or what? Again, the goal is not necessarily to entertain runners, but to get them back on the road.

Speaking of getting back on the road, it probably goes without saying that someone needs to give women's running a boost. One possible direction—I'm just thinking out loud here—involves a store that sells lightweight polypropylene jogging bras. You know, those colorful ones that have become so popular around the running circuit. It would be the first store of its kind, staffed entirely by experienced female runners, catering only to a woman's jogging bra needs.

My wife likes the idea. Actually, she's crazy about it. She thinks we could make a fortune. According to her, there's nothing in the world more difficult to find than a good jogging bra. Hardly anybody carries them.

I'm glad she's so enthusiastic. To show my gratitude, I'll probably make her manager of the store. In fact, I might even let her name the place.

Someone's going to have to. I wouldn't touch that job if the future of running depended on it.

Star Trek: The Running Shoe Peril

Captain Kirk: "Captain's log, star date 013093. Beamed up running shoes from planet Earth. Unable to comprehend proper usage of scientifically designed and engineered athletic footwear. Chekov, where are the laces on this shoe?"

Chekov: "I don't know, Keptin. The technology is unbelievable. It looks as though the shoes can either be inflated with the pump button or a disposable CO_2 cartridge. Will you be using them for shipboard speed work or interplanetary ultras?"

Uhura: "Captain, I'm getting indications of a Klingon presence."

Kirk: "Mr. Spock?"

Spock: "I confirm several Imperial Klingon warships, Captain. They're heading toward our position at Warp 7."

Kirk: "No, the CO_2 cartridge. Where do I insert it?"

Spock: "Might I suggest, Captain, that we first remove ourselves to a more secure sector and then address the matter of your running shoes? That would be the most logical approach."

Kirk: "There's nothing logical about these shoes. Look at this design. Look at the styling. Chekov, how many times should I depress the pump button?"

Chekov: "Keptin?"

Kirk: "The pump. Is two times enough? Three? For God's sake, don't these things come with an instruction manual?"

Chekov: "Instruction manuals are no longer required, Keptin. Running shoes are as central to American culture as their cars were in the 1990s."

Sulu: "Captain, I'm having difficulty holding course."

Kirk: "Secure all stations. Shut down main engines. Sulu, you have the con. Chekov, take a look at this. What function do you think leaving out a full third of the middle sole appears to have?"

Chekov: "It's beyond my comprehension, Keptin. It may be that earthlings have discovered that taking out the material subtracts 1.5 ounces from each shoe. Or maybe they found that when you run, the middle part of the sole serves little purpose. So why put cushioning there?"

Spock: "Captain, the Klingons are firing their photon torpedoes."

Kirk: "Engineering."

Scotty: "Aye, Captain?"

Kirk: "Mr. Scott, we're testing running shoes up here. Put us on full deflector power."

Scotty: "I canna guarantee the deflectors, Captain. Our defense systems are already overloaded."

Chekov: "Keptin, I think I've got the pump figured out."

Kirk: "Good work, Chekov!"

Chekov: "Except I'm not exactly sure where the air is going."

Kirk: "Damn! Analysis, Mr. Spock."

Spock: "It would appear, Captain, that the shoe has a skeleton-like bladder which, when inflated with the pump button or a disposable CO_2 cartidge, holds your foot quite securely in place."

Kirk: "What are you saying, Spock?"

Spock: "I'm saying, Captain, that this may well be the most advanced running shoe in the galaxy. I suggest you treat it as such."

Kirk: "It's diabolical!"

Spock: "On the contrary, it's perfectly logical. Earthlings have shoe technology that reaches the limits of the universe."

Kirk: "What I would like is an explanation for the use of these shoes, not the evolution of the running shoe."

Chekov: "What's the next move, Keptin?"

Kirk: "The question is, is there a next move?"

Spock: "There is a way, Captain."

Kirk: "Spit it out, Spock."

Spock: "Teenage earthlings are rumored to excel in the knowledge of basketball, popular music and athletic footwear."

Kirk: "Chekov, do we have any teenagers on board?"

Chekov: "Yes sir. There's one in the game room."

Kirk: "Radio down and ask him to provide me with the required information."

Spock: "By my estimation, Captain, it would take the teenager more than the one minute and 30 seconds that we have for him to decode the secrets of your shoes. Our deflector shield is almost out of power."

Dr. McCoy: "Jim, you know I hate to agree with Spock, but he's right. The *Enterprise* is in danger. You can't sacrifice hundreds of lives over a pair of running shoes. You've got to get us out of here!"

Kirk: "I know my responsibilities, Bones. But I also know that sometimes you've got to take a chance. These aren't just any old running shoes. We may be witnessing a birth here. Possibly the next step in our own evolution. We've got to see this mission through."

Uhura: "Captain, it worked. I've just received a response from the game room."

Kirk: "I knew he could do it! Bridge to engine room. Deflector shields down. I'll have Warp 9."

Scotty: "Aye, Captain."

Spock: "It appears that your intuitiveness on earthling teenage behavior has saved the ship, Captain. Congratulations are in order."

Kirk: "Don't thank me, Spock. The real thanks goes to that teenager in the game room. Without him all would have been lost. Uhura, play back the transmission."

Uhura: "Yes, sir."

From the intercom comes static, a dinging of pinballs, loud music in the background. An unintelligible voice speaks.

Kirk: "Translation, Spock."

Spock: "The dialect is most unfamiliar, Captain, but if I'm correct he seems to be quoting from an ancient Earth corporate slogan."

Kirk: "Don't keep me in suspense, Spock. What did he say?"

Spock: "The translation reads...Just Do It."

I CAN SEE CLEARLY NOW

Observations on running and runners

Running Styles

While going through my mail the other day, I noticed a picture in a magazine that was purported to be a group of runners. The individuals portrayed were all neat, clean, and beaming with happy smiles as they came sprinting up a chip-covered trail.

"Those aren't runners, they're fashion models," I told my wife.

Always keen to assimilate my wisdom on such matters, she fixed me with an intense look. "Did you eat all the ice cream?" she asked, "there's nothing in the carton."

"Well, first of all," I explained patiently, "they look too fresh and cheerful, whereas real runners are generally rumpled, sweaty, and straining with fatigue. Second, they're training on a chip-covered trail instead of dodging cars, trucks and potholes. What really gives them away, though, is that they're *sprinting*. No self-respecting runner I know would ever be caught dead sprinting."

"You even ate all of the apple pie!" my wife shouted.

This enlightening exchange got me to thinking that there are probably many people like my wife who have waited in vain for someone to erase their ignorance concerning proper running styles. Since this is a subject that I've analyzed as earnestly as Socrates contemplated existence, I herewith offer as a public service the following compendium of the basic styles of running.

The Ultramarathoner's Crawl

Ultramarathoners, being generally optimistic souls, will start off a workout at a brisk 12-minute pace, which they will maintain for approximately 10 steps. Then they shift into the standard ultramarathoner's crawl. One foot is raised and placed six inches forward on the road. The ultramarathoner then breathes deeply, tests his pulse, adjusts his fanny pack, takes a sip of Body-Fuel replacement drink, and checks his watch.

And he repeats the process.

A good ultramarathoner, if he had a pillow handy, could take a nap between steps. His forward motion defies detection by the naked eye. Nevertheless, his progress is steady and unrelenting, and during the course of a day he will traverse entire states.

How does he do it? No one is really quite sure, but the tale of the tortoise and the hare leaps instantly to mind.

The Sunday Jogger's Saunter

The Sunday jogger prefers workout clothes with a bit of dash: hot pink workout suits, bright orange Lycra tights, and antifreeze green headbands. The astutely coiffed and color-uncoordinated Sunday jogger dresses as though perspiration would be the kiss of death.

Although it's not unusual to see a whole group of Sunday joggers sauntering along together, it is rare to see them communicating. They prefer to plug in their Walkmans, turn the volume up to Madonna, and vogue off down the road.

Their style of running is characterized by quick, tiny steps, an exaggerated straight vertical posture, and a facial expression combining equal parts of pride and suffering.

For cross-training, the Sunday jogger prefers classes in body awareness, Yoga, stretching, meditation, relaxation and ballet. When they run, they seek that special feeling in the mind that represents the creation of alpha waves.

They seldom, if ever, achieve it.

The typical workout for a Sunday jogger has the average life span of a trout-stream fly hatch. It consists of getting dressed, running once around the block, coming home, and arguing about television programs. This once-a-week Herculean expenditure of energy does serve a purpose, however. It entitles the Sunday jogger to rush out and purchase yet another article of fluorescent running gear with which to startle friends and frighten neighborhood dogs.

The Ten-Mile-A-Day Shuffler

Of all the types of runners, this one is most predictable. The 10-mile-a-day shuffler is programmed to run a given number of miles come hell or high water. He runs in sweltering heat with parched tongue and in torrential rain with cars and buses belching carcinogens in his face. His form always remains the same—stiff and clunky, like spilling a can of Tinkertoys, as though he is suffering from a wound you cannot see. His pace never differs. Even the location of his run is unvarying. Nothing is more important to the 10-mile-a-day shuffler than, well...getting in those 10 miles a day.

When you work out with the 10-mile-a-day shuffler there is a temptation to be overwhelmed by your partner's unswerving devotion to duty. There is an even greater temptation to throw the pace off, cut the run short, run in a new location—in general, throw a wrench into the works. The 10-mile-a-day shuffler, however, will be swayed by nothing, conveying the impression of being in a trance of sufficient depth that it cannot be penetrated by even your vile epithets.

The Look-Easy Loper

Basically, this style of running implies casualness. The look-easy loper thinks he is being watched, and wants everyone to believe he's in excellent shape. Therefore, he never warms up. As soon as his feet hit the pavement he's moving. Fast.

The look-easy loper enjoys running in parks and byways, or wherever there is an audience. He weaves through foot traffic and surges around automobiles with no trouble. He charges up flights of stairs in a blur of speed. On his face is an expression of almost insufferable self-satisfaction. And cheerfulness.

Underneath it all, however, the look-easy loper is suffering. Big-time. He has heel spurs and blood blisters. His Achilles tendon is torn, and his knees are empty of cartilage but filling with flakes of kneecap that grind in the joint like Rice Krispies. His right hamstring is so tight it feels like a guitar string that's been tuned several octaves past its normal pitch. His toenails are in various stages of coming and going, either shiny pink little nubbins or hideous black things. But the look-easy loper is strong. He *never* complains about pain.

Not until he gets home, anyway.

As soon as the look-easy loper is safely inside his house, he will immediately start moaning and groaning. His spouse will be asked to fetch ice packs, prepare hot baths, give massages, and generally listen to more whining and complaining than any normal person should ever have to.

This pathetic behavior will continue until the following morning when, like one of those dung-colored lizards that can look like orchids whenever they feel like it, he will bound out of bed and head off down the street, smiling, and making it look easy.

The Competitive Strider

Ragged sweatshirt, dog-chewed gym trunks, dirty running shoes purchased in the previous century—Neotatterism might best describe this runner. Looks aren't important to the competitive strider, at least not when compared to a fast 10K time. The competitive strider is a workhorse. He is as at home on a track as he is on a treadmill. He probably descended from a hamster.

He never misses a workout, lest he find his times dropping, or his finishing place in a race not what it should be. You can find him running at anytime: before funerals, after weddings, and during visits by his mother-in-law. Nothing gets in the way of his workout.

To the competitive strider, every workout is a race. No one goes by him unchallenged. If another runner pulls alongside, the competitive strider will surge ahead of his adversary and not slack up until the competition has been sufficiently destroyed.

What happens when the competitive strider is passed during a workout? He falls to the ground, kicking, screaming and sunfishing, until the people from the Padded Palace come and take him away.

And what happens when the competitive strider meets his match in a race?

Believe me, you don't want to know.

No tears, please, for the competitive strider. It's a waste of good suffering. Besides, his problem is nothing an ice bath, some wet sheets, a frontal lobotomy, and electroshock treatments can't cure.

There are literally dozens of other styles of running. After studying them for a while you'll be able to spot most of them with little or no trouble. The important thing to remember, however, is that whenever you see someone sprinting up a chip path, looking neat and clean, and smiling from ear to ear, it's probably not a runner. At least not a self-respecting one.

Dressed To Chill

Sure, this is dumb, but there. It's out in the open. Stiff, bulky and cumbersome.

Rain gear.

The stuff is still brand new. It's been hiding in the back of my closet ever since I bought it. That's because I don't really enjoy running in the rain. Actually, I hate it. There's something about splashing down the street with sleet and stinging hail whipping my face while the rest of humanity moves from one warm shelter to another, from work to car to home, like prairie dogs scurrying from mound to mound, that makes me steam like a geyser, that makes my gorge rise up like lava from a long-dormant volcano.

If that's too many geographical metaphors for you, tough. That's the kind of mood I'm in. A mean mood. A spitting mood. The righteously perfect mood, I think, in which to convince myself to go running in a storm.

I'm only doing this out of sheer frustration. We've had a full week of steady, ulcerous rain. Seven days of being holed up in the house in a state of acute inertia, forced TV and related garbage. If I don't get outside soon, I'll go bananas.

I'll just crack open the front door and...brr! Look at it come down. Maybe I'll wait a bit. I just can't go thundering off into the street, trumpeting and kicking up water. A person needs time to think these things out. After all, it is midwinter. Most things are sleeping, gathering their sap for the big push, marking time, living off their borrowed fat, cocooning their way to the coming warmth that the tilting planet will soon bring. Besides, I wouldn't want to get my running shoes wet. They absorb not only moisture but 85% of my yearly income.

Let's see, what can I do to kill some time? I can do the dishes. I can read a book. I can hook myself up to an IV drip of daytime television. I can hang myself with the cord from the Venetian blind. That's what I really feel like doing.

Maybe I'll lie down for a few minutes. Just a quick nap to rev up my REMs. That's all I need. A tiny dream and then I'm on my way.

Wait a minute, what would my wife do if she came home and found me napping? I know what she'll do. She'll give me one of those you-poor-fool smiles, the kind of merciless grin you might see on the face of a Marine drill instructor hectoring a naive recruit, and then she'll shout, "Enough snacking! Enough comfort! Enough excuse-making! It's time to get out and kick some asphalt. Go get wet!"

Sure, easy for her to say. She'll be languishing, high and dry, on the couch, snoring like a gas-powered weed-whacker. I'll be the guy with the wet feet, the clenched teeth, the head-to-toe goose-bumps. I'll be the one running sneaky-Pete style, so as not to attract a lightning bolt.

What I need is some kind of motivation, a source of inspiration, a good reason to run. What I need is some fool who's willing to brave this awful weather with me. I'll call one of my friends.

Let's see, Bob can meet from 4:30 p.m. to 6:00 p.m. on Monday, Wednesday and the second Saturday of every month. Charlie can meet from 3:15 p.m. to 5:30 p.m. on Tuesdays and Thursdays and on Sundays from 8:00 a.m. to 9:00 a.m., and Dan can meet every other Friday from noon to...

Forget it. Finding a running partner is like trying to get the Nile to flow south.

I'm told that some runners don't mind the rain. They enjoy it! They luxuriate in a downpour, shower in a thunderstorm. They smile as they get soaked to the skin. Personally, I think such behavior summarizes the flaky and irrational mental state of goons, goofs and other low-rent runners. Whenever I see a dark cloud overhead, I start to shiver violently and the words "head for cover" pop unbidden into my mind.

Which is unfortunate, especially since it rains so much around here. You don't believe me? Listen to that thunder. Check out the lightning. Sidewalks stay wet around here. Roadways become duck ponds. Smart runners like me stay inside.

I'll bet the Japanese run in the rain. Japanese workers, as you've heard, do their jobs as if their jobs depended on it. They work hard and I bet they run hard, too. Even when it's raining. And me? Here I sit, high and dry, while my muscles atrophy and my waistline grows until my belt makes me look like one of those segmented insects. If we're ever going to beat the Japanese at their own game, I'd better get on the ball.

I'm going to give it just a few more minutes, though. It looks like the storm might be breaking up.

Who am I kidding? It hasn't let up a drop. I'm just running out of excuses, that's my problem. I need some kind of excuse Rolodex.

I'm trying to muster up my courage. Really, I am. But no matter how steely my commitment is, every time I peek out the window my discipline starts to slide. Can you blame me? Just look at those clouds! Blue-black clouds, the color of a bad bruise. Bullying, operatic, Wagnerian clouds, all low, ominous rumbles and thundering crescendos.

Really, I'm about to get moving. I'm making remedial resolutions even as we speak, but human beings don't stop on a dime. It takes time to bring the stately ship of running around on a new tack. Besides, I can't go right this second. It's coming down in buckets out there. Raindrops the size of a quarter. An orange. A cantaloupe!

Maybe I should drop this sport and take up a more sensible and practical obsession—like earning a million dollars, for example, or acquiring a brace of Purdeys.

Okay, okay, I'm going. But if you want my opinion, this is nut stuff. I'm pulling on my gloves. I'm lacing up my shoes. I'm stepping into my *eewwwww* rainwear.

Wait a minute! There's the phone! Whew. Talk about *dues ex machina*.

It's my kid. He wants a ride home from school. He doesn't want to get wet. Sheeesh! Can you believe it? Afraid to go out in the rain. I thought kids were supposed to be tough. Sometimes I wonder about this younger generation. Heck, when I was his age, I never let a little storm slow me down. No way. I played in hurricanes. I walked home in tornadoes. I was wet all the time. But it was a good kind of wet. The kind of wet that soaks right through to your bones and makes your nose run like a faucet.

Memories like those, they're enough to last a lifetime.

You Might Be A Runner If...

Lots of people run, but only a select handful are runners. The guy who laces up his Reeboks once a month to run to the Circle K doesn't qualify. Neither does the hot shot with the $3,000 treadmill in his garage and the closet full of Nike running gear.

Sure, you have to run to be a runner. But in my book you also have to be passionate—okay, certifiably insane—about all things connected with the sport. You live and love running, you respect it, you spread the gospel of running, but you never forget it's mostly about fun. Being a runner is as much a state of mind as a state of fitness.

No set rules exist to determine who's a runner and who isn't. But I put my team of experts to work and came up with 27 experiences that define this special breed. Call them runs of passage, if you will.

And don't worry if you haven't accomplished all of them. Few people have. Maybe no one. Think of the list as a series of worthy goals to achieve before you pass on to that big run in the sky. So, with apologies to Jeff Foxworthy, you *might* be a runner if:

—You own the video *Chariots of Fire.*

—You've turned on a spouse, friend, kid or neighbor to running.

—You wear out shoes faster than your five-year old.

—You take the stairs to your 18th-floor office, even when the elevator is working.

—You can convert miles into kilometers with no effort.

—Your medicine cabinet contains more anti-inflammatory medication than the local drug store.

—You are skinny enough to induce spontaneous intestinal discomfort in unwary onlookers just by removing your sweats.

—You realize that any conversation can be artfully steered to the subject of marathoning.

—You've run Boston more times than John Kelley.

—You forget your kids' birthdays, but remember the exact mile splits for every marathon you've run.

—You would rather get up at 5:00 a.m. to go running than you would sleep in.

—You realize that you'll never have to buy another T-shirt for the rest of your life.

—You're not very nice to be around when you're tapering for a race.

—You know more about running shoes than the salesman does.

—You won't spend $20 on lawn mower repairs, but you'll fork out $100 for a new heart rate monitor.

—You look at everything in terms of how it might affect your next race.

—You check your pulse several times a day.

—Your friends ask your advice on running.

—You'd restrict yourself to eating tubers and drinking branch water if you thought it would get you a PR.

—You actually seek out steep hills on your training runs.

—You're in bed by 9:00 p.m. every night, and you're single.

—All you ever receive at Christmas is running clothes.

—Your dog refuses to accompany you on your long runs.

—Your race T-shirts are more precious to you than the Magna Carta, the Shroud of Turin and the Hope Diamond combined.

—You risk your job for an extra 15 minutes of workout time during lunch break.

—You run in weather that even the postman wouldn't brave.

—You have a positive outlook on life, and it's all because of the sport of running.

The Uncool Runner

I was beginning to train for marathons, putting in 120-mile weeks, long runs and mile repeats on the track, really getting in shape. Now I hear that marathons are O-U-T—out. No one is running them anymore. Anyone who runs a step over 10K is a certifiable loony from the bottom bin.

When did this happen?

Nobody ever tells me anything. I just went out and bought a new watch. Now I hear that the kind of watch I purchased is a collector's item. Everyone else is wearing a $250 Polar ACCurex Heart Rate Monitor. Even though a watch like mine with a second hand and a carotid artery will do.

For years I've been pinning my race numbers on the old-fashioned way—with pins. Now I'm told that the truly cool runner is using InSport Race Elastic, which allows you to attach your race number to a waistband instead of pinning it to your singlet. The convenience escapes me.

All my life, I've somehow managed to be out of the room when the new trends were announced. Everybody's on to new running fabrics like Microdenier, Polartec, Spandura and Tensilite. I still wear cotton shorts. I don't even know what Tensilite is, let alone what it does.

My wife says it's like stock tips. Once you get one, it's too late. I showed up at a race in my "Planet Reebok" T-shirt, feeling almost hip, and the first person I see informs me that my T-shirt is little more than a pathetic foray into fashion hell. "Get with the picture," he said, showing me his 'Run for Bosnia' T-shirt. "This is what everyone is wearing."

Truly cool runners somehow mysteriously know these things. They keep up on the latest sartorial trends. So do I. I leaf through running magazines, read the articles and think, "How interesting, this is what the elite runners are doing." Cool runners attend races and talk to other runners. I do too. But somehow, they are in the know. I never seem to realize that my singlets have the labels on the inside. Or that I'm wearing my baseball cap, bill forward. Then someone gives me a quizzical look, and I have to glance around and make sure they're not filming one of those "Stay In School" public service spots.

All runners I know are using a $30 piece of plastic to stretch out their calves when I'm still using a wall. Any wall. Six months later I think, "Okay, I'll give one of those plastic calf stretchers a try," and it's too late. The crowd is already on to something else.

I am so uncool that even when I'm cool it somehow doesn't look right, like when I run on the track. I'll be doing 440s when other runners are doing 880s. By the time I start doing 880s, everyone is doing mile repeats. (Is even calling one lap around the track a 440 uncool?)

I could make a virtue of being uncool. It's not that I don't have a clue what shoes runners are wearing today. It's that I love my sneakers. (Oops! Sorry. Not sneakers. Athletic shoes. Sneakers is the kind of dumb word that someone uses when they just refuse to understand.) I own a pair of P.F. Flyers. Everyone else has the latest and the greatest—athletic shoes that light up and blow up. I know that my P.F. Flyers are more offensive than bad breath or right-wing politics, but they are a symbol—I refuse to change to another brand until there's world peace. I wear cotton clothes, not because I never heard of Tensilite, but because my life is so rich and compelling.

Or I could come clean and admit that I could care less. Being hopelessly out of step means I get to act like I want and wear what I want. There's plenty of room away from the crowd. I pull on my shoes. I don't want to pump them up. And I may not have a $30 piece of plastic to stretch with, but I have my choice of buildings.

By the way, I was just getting used to the taste of ERG. When did everybody switch to Cytomax?

The Art Of Resting

I used to think of Sisyphus, the mythological king who was punished in Hades by repeatedly having to roll a huge stone up a hill only to have it roll back down again, as sort of the patron saint of competitive runners. That is, competitive running is a heavy stone and demands a steady labor to keep it rolling, and every time it falls back, so does the level of your conditioning. For years I adhered strongly to this philosophy. A day without running was unthinkable—worse than a death in the family. My life was completely geared to my daily workout.

Lately, though, I feel I have been overlooking the true instruction of Sisyphus' life, which is that each time his great grindstone rolls to the bottom of the mountain, he is granted a rest, while he walks back down to retrieve it. Though he must work for all time, according to the myth, he does not work all the time.

Nor, I decided recently, should I.

Having just completed my 785th consecutive day of running 10 miles a day, every day, I suddenly hit a wall I had never hit in my life as a runner. Burnout. The thought of another 10-mile run was nearly enough to buckle my knees. As it was, in the waning days of my streak, I pulled myself out the door each morning as though I were a zombie on the way to my own beheading.

That's when I decided it was time for a break. In fact, I decided to extend the spirit of the Sabbath to outlandish proportions by taking a few months off. I wanted to see what it would feel like not to run, to exist in a kind of creative idleness that an acquaintance of mine calls "power lounging."

It was a heroic challenge. I had been running for so long, I wasn't sure I could stop. Even my family was alarmed. During those first days when I didn't run, they stopped everything they were doing and hollered, "Aren't you missing your workout?"

And my fellow runners? When I first told them about my planned three-month hiatus, they looked at me in the kind of alarmed awe Japanese actors reserve for Godzilla. "Stop running? For three months? How could you?" With my friends there's a line drawn in the sand. Either you're compulsive or you're not. Which side of the line did I stand on? I was about to find out.

On the first day without running, I woke up, put my face in my hands and started to weep. From simply weeping, I moved onto sobbing. From sobbing, I graduated to dry heaving. Then, totally spent, I sat in silence for the remainder of the day.

On the second day my grief deepened. Two full days without running! Already I felt my conditioning sinking back into the primordial ooze.

Day three was horrible. I began to lose control of all my bodily functions, even the enjoyable ones. Steam started to pour out of my ears, my arms began to spin around wildly like needles on a pressure gauge, and my head began to shudder violently and make a delightful cooing sound.

Day four. I stopped hating myself in the morning and, instead, waited until late in the afternoon.

By day five my mood swings were enormous. I was on a run-less roller coaster, complete with plunges, buildups and twisting turns akin to the denial, anger and depression that make up the three of the four stages of grief. All that was missing was the final stage—recovery.

On the sixth day my gloom finally decamped, leaving me in an irritatingly cheerful sort of mood—impervious to comments by other runners. It was like seeing daylight after spending a week in a mineshaft. I was going to make it after all!

Over the next few weeks, as the days crawled by like a snail, I took great long walks by the sea, spent time with my family, caught up on the yard work and stopped postponing jury duty. Once again, life was full of possibilities. I was more laid-back than a macrobiotic checkout clerk at a health food store.

Toward the end of my running hiatus I had a pivotal dream. A Zen monk gave me a large block of wood to sand down to nothing. As I neared the end, and began to look forward to the project's completion, the monk came back and took my sandpaper away, telling me to use only my fingernails. The point, he said, was the process, not the goal. Every life ends the same way, I understood him to be implying—the hero always dies—so why be in such a hurry to get to the finish line?

The day after my dream, I succumbed to the enticing lure of a warm spring afternoon and started running again. But since that day, my attitude has changed. Now, I enjoy myself when I run. I take slow jogs by the sea. I run in the forests. And sometimes I don't even run at all.

I not only discovered that I can stop running for months at a time and my life doesn't crumble, but that having my nose to the grindstone, day after day, is not always the most beneficial position for a runner. Sometimes lying on the couch is.

Sex, Lies And Running

It had to happen sooner or later. Madison Avenue has discovered running. And how are they popularizing it? Go ahead. Take a guess.

That's right, with sex. They've got the running magazines full of articles about how sexy running is. There are stories about how running makes you love better, last longer and find more partners. Already enough articles have been written on the subject to sink a fleet of luxury liners.

One can only hope this fad will pass quickly so that serious runners can get back to what's important—being tired, grumpy and concerned with PRs. Running is a sport of getting in shape, not of selecting a date.

Now look what Madison Avenue is saying.

"Go for a run," they advise, "then look in the mirror when you get home. You're slim, healthy and fit. You're a runner, and you've never been sexier."

Oh right. Like I'm really excited by a woman who says, "Oh, my God, I think I just pulled a hamstring." Like she's turned on by the odor of Icy-Hot.

It's pretty obvious that those ad executives have never been on a 10-mile run before. Running makes you hot, tired and sweaty. Oh sure, it makes you feel good, but not sexy. Sexy is the wrong word. In fact, sex is probably the last thing on your mind after a run. Something cold to drink? You bet. A few hours in the recliner? Now you're talking. But *sex?* Give me a break.

Why do the ad people think running is sexy? Is it the clothes? Lycra is definitely in and tight clothes seem to come with the territory. They're colorful too. Even people who don't run are wearing Lycra. They wear it to the mall, they wear it to the supermarket, they wear it when they go to dinner. They wear it everywhere except on a run, because that would get it all smelly.

The running magazines are full of ads of men and women in these tight clothes. They're even on the covers. The attractive models are in mid-stride, hair flying, smiles pasted on their faces. Like all models, they don't sweat, but they know how to make the girl or guy who bought the magazine sweat.

It's getting so a person has to flip through the magazine just to be sure it's okay to take it home.

Sex is fantasy but running sure isn't. Running is pitting all your strength against the competition during a race. Running is squeezing over to the guard rail on a narrow road so a Mack truck can go by. Running is being chased down a country lane by a mongrel dog who guards his half-acre of yard like a little Caesar.

Sex is what you read about in the running magazines after the running is over.

Now for the statistics. One magazine survey of runners found that almost 80 percent of them said running makes them better lovers, while 79 percent said that runners were more sexually attractive than nonrunners. One runner in five said that he or she had "gotten intimate" during a race.

Intimate? During a race? When your legs are like lead, your breath is coming on like a death rattle and your face is coated with perspiration and other unmentionables?

Men look terrible coming across the finish line. Women don't look much better. Most of them look like they're posing for a 50-cent piece.

"Look at you, you're all sweaty," my wife told me the other day after I came in from a run. I gave her a hug, and she pushed me away. "Yuck," she said. "Go take a shower."

Like I said, if you want to read a book about sex and running, you've got to buy two separate books.

Murphy's Law. . .
As Applied To Running

Let's suppose just for a moment that the optimistic Murphy had been a runner...

No matter how long or hard you shop for new running shoes, after you've bought them, they will be on sale elsewhere, cheaper.

When you finally locate that perfect running shoe, the model will be discontinued.

Any free refreshments will have been consumed immediately prior to your finish in a race.

A training partner will either be much faster or much slower than you.

A race official will estimate the number of portable toilets needed for a given race and order half that many.

A shortcut in any training run is always up the steepest mountain.

In some states a "runner's high" is considered a criminal offense.

At a party, all smoke will drift directly into the face of the nearest runner.

A cold or flu will be contracted the day before the most important race of the year.

In a race, you will forget to start or stop your watch, depending on which you remembered to do.

The doctor has never seen a knee injury quite as bad as your's before.

When nothing can stop you from attaining a PR, something will.

It is a breech of etiquette to consume cold beer within eye shot of an ongoing marathon.

On the command "Go" you will notice your shoelaces are untied.

If you drop from a race due to exhaustion, you will have to walk in anyway.

You will always finish one place out of the medals in your age group.

Two large rocks could accomplish the same as the $19.95 pair of Heavy Hands you just purchased.

A dog will attack a runner only when it is least expected to do so.

Upon completion of your first sub-three hour marathon, the course will be found to be inaccurately measured.

By the time you reach the marathon aid station at 25 miles, everyone will have gone home.

Anyone injured and unable to run will be shunned by fellow runners as though they were carriers of an infectious disease.

When preparing to overtake and pass a competitor, you will, in turn, be passed.

All smokers know someone who died from running.

There is always an excuse for not running well; if you run well, all excuses are null and void.

If everything seems to be going well in a race, you obviously don't know what's going on.

If you ever do win a race, the shock will lay you up for months.

Tuning-Up

I love running. I can't imagine anyone liking it more than I do. I enjoy every wonderful thing about it; the training, the racing and especially the fine company of other runners. And, of course, I enjoy the way it makes me feel—an early morning run along a forest path or an afternoon jog along the beach can give me more goose bumps than nude skydiving. But there is one thing about running that I don't enjoy. Sometimes, not often mind you, just every once in awhile, I have what you might call "a bad day."

When I have a bad day, I'm tired before I even get started. On a bad day, my legs feel like they belong to a comedian, rubber jointed and useless for everything but pratfalls. On a bad day it takes every form of discipline I know just to pull myself out the front door. On a bad day, I struggle through the entire workout, constantly wrestling with a craven urge to stop. On a bad day, time slows down to the most creaking rattletrap pace. And on a bad day, my mind wanders, legs and muscles protest and depression grows until I feel completely without purpose. A planet without a sun, revolving in darkness.

Mental fatigue. Lack of drive. Low biorhythms. Call it what you want. To a runner, a bad day is the essence of horror. Not the acute horror of a bomb blast or plane crash, mercifully brief, but a chronic horror that has a way of infecting your whole day, and making you feel like someone popped the pull tab on your brain and let all the fizz out.

Scary stuff, huh? Hang on, it gets worse. A bad day, like no other phenomenon, can force the average runner to discard high and lofty aspirations, to instantly break training and miss a day...a week...even a month of running. What follows is piteous beyond mortal comprehension. Skills fade. Muscle memory atrophies. Even dreams, once haven to fine long-distance workouts, become impoverished by empty, joyless days. Go to work, take the money, pay the bills. Life as a runless hell.

But if you're a serious runner, or someone like me who, when not training, picks up pounds the way a shaggy dog picks up fleas, taking time off is *not* a valid solution to a bad day—or even a *horrible* day, for that matter. For us, there must be some other, more creative method of preserving our sanity and maintaining our conditioning.

There is, and it's called music.

How can music shift you into a higher gear and get you on the road again? Easy. Let's say that during a workout you start to feel pain. You might think, 'I feel horrible,' or 'I'm getting a stitch.' As your mind begins to focus on the pain, it becomes bigger, and as the pain becomes the focal point, the mind gives it more and more attention until it takes command of desire. Music can help you absorb the pain instead of focusing on it. You perceive the exercise as less intensive and your body reacts biochemically.

Still not convinced?

Exercising with music is nothing new. Look at how well music has worked in the past. Primitive African tribes planted and harvested crops to a beat, a specific tempo. And ever since there's been a military, there has been marching music. Even NASA has astronauts exercise while listening to music. Throughout history, music has been used as an incentive to exercise and a way to promote compliance with a routine.

Need scientific proof?

Research has shown that music and rhythm stimulate movement and improve coordination. A study done at Ohio State University found that people who work out with music have significantly lower levels of beta-endorphin, the natural opiate the brain releases in response to stress or pain.

Of course, music won't work for everyone. Some runners are fussier than the bouncers at Studio 54. They shun music because they prefer to focus on pain and use it to motivate themselves. They believe that if you're a serious athlete, music can inhibit your ability to concentrate. And if you don't concentrate, you can't maximize your potential.

Other runners are concerned about the physical danger involved in running while listening to music. Like traffic, for instance. They worry that they won't hear the Peterbilt truck bearing down on them and then—WHACKO! I hope you have enough dental fillings to ensure identification.

They're absolutely right. They're as right as rainwater. Running with music can be dangerous and I wouldn't advise any music-aided runners to take to the roads until they understand the basic precautions which need to be taken. Most of these precautions are just good common sense: wear the kind of headphones that let outside sound in; keep the volume on your radio or cassette low; run facing traffic; steer toward mercifully deserted streets if possible; stick to the sidewalks as much as you can; double-check each intersection before darting across. The long and short of it is: When running with music, be more alert than ever.

There are also a number of runners who are worried about how others might perceive them as a music-aided runner. These people wouldn't be caught dead with one of those pseudo-athletic geegaws strapped to their head—it might elicit stares. Friends might think that they've drifted off into the oblivion of the valley of the casual runner. But if music makes you feel good, isn't that what matters? If it helps make your running less tedious and more pleasant, isn't that what's important?

Thinking about tuning up? Not sure about what kind of music to listen to? No problem. Whether you prefer rock, jazz, country and western or a Swiss yodel, the "right" music is purely a matter of taste. Music with a predictable rhythm is nice, but I've had some of my best workouts while listening to everything from Bach to Bruce Springsteen. Today's lightweight radio headsets are cheap, unobtrusive once you get used to them, and they allow you to avoid choosing between running and relaxing to your favorite music.

What more could you ask? If you really want to enjoy your running, simply try changing your audio environment. Music is guaranteed to inject variety into your running and cure your "bad days" once and for all.

The Initial Track Workout

While warming up on the track the other day, I overheard two runners discussing their workout schedule. There was much in the way of talk about SW, RPR, PT and RL.

Now, I understood exactly what those guys were saying, but I could tell by the bewildered expression of several other runners who were standing nearby that the exchange made these two runners sound like they worked for an agency such as the CIA, FBI, NCAA, AOC or USATF.

In the fast-paced life of track workouts, where rest is short and hearts beat as fast as those of hummingbirds, there just isn't time to mouth out, "You slowed down on that lap," so we track runners shorten it to YSDOTL. Therefore, athletes are often forced to communicate through laconic signals, minimalist gestures and sprinter's acronyms.

In an effort to enlighten those new to speed workouts, I've compiled a list of the most common acronyms and initials used by track athletes with little or no breath to spare:

SW: Speedwork.
RPR: Resting pulse rate.
PT: Pain threshold.
RL: Recovery lap.
IHSW: I hate SW.
QCIGFY: Quit complaining, it's good for you.
OLGTOW: Okay, let's get this over with.
H15X440STY: How's 15x440 sound to you?
ISI: It sounds impossible.
YWTGISDY: You want to get in shape, don't you?
IGS: I guess so.
PPPHMHWGL: Puff, puff, puff. How many have we got left?
TWTWUL: That was the warm-up lap.
OGH: Oh God. Help!
WTDYGOTO: What time did you get on that one?
IFTSMW: I forgot to set my watch.
COYFB: Come on, you're falling behind.
HHHWILYTMIT: Huff, huff, huff. Why'd I let you talk me into this?
AYRAYPT: Are you running at your PT?

MLMDT: More like my death threshold.

DLD: Don't lie down.

ICYOTNRLO: I'll catch you on the next RL, okay?

AYR: Are you ready?

ITATRWG: Is that all the rest we get?

WYRPR: What's your RPR?

IDKICCTH: I don't know. I can't count that high.

OFMTG: Only five more to go.

MAWBFH: Might as well be five hundred.

LSUOTO: Let's speed up on this one.

WWW: Wheeze, wheeze, wheeze.

GJ: Good job.

AWD: Are we done?

OM: One more.

GG: Gasp, gasp!

TIWF: That's it. We're finished.

TG: Thank God.

GTFOM: Got time for one more?

ISLMHOFATTRHDOTF: I'd sooner light my hair on fire and try to roast hot dogs over the flames.

Running Advice For The President

Dear Bubba,

Pardon me for saying so, but you seem a little depressed lately. As moody as an album of Billy Holliday's greatest hits. It's your job, isn't it? It's lonely at the top. Especially since Monica doesn't stop by anymore. Your popularity rating has gone down, too. That's not good. Your constituents are calling you a draft-dodging, sax-blowing, fork-tongued, no-inhaling, burger-biting, weenie-waving president. They say you're a very good candidate for the centerfold in *Psychology Today*.

Well, I've got a solution to all your problems. I'd like to usher you back into a new and better world: the world of running. Think of me as your shrink, here to facilitate your running program. My advice, in a nutshell: keep it simple, keep it fun, and remember that even a bad day running beats a good day with the chief advisor (that little guy in your pants). Here are a few tips:

Set Some Goals. If you can stare down that evil and amoral dictator, Saddam Hussein, surely you can deal with a log book. Embark on a mission. Run every day, rain or shine. Get your heart rate up to the point where it can be measured by an EKG from a dozen feet away. You're not going to get in shape by switching to light beer and watching Jazzercize on TV...or bonding with interns. Get out of touch. Let the world know there are times when you cannot be reached. Your focus should be: Cancel my meetings. Call me tomorrow. I'm going for a workout. And don't worry about being missed. Who's gonna miss someone they can't catch?

Run Faster. Book it, Mr. President. Pick up the pace. Sweat. It's important to glisten. You have the waistline like a Beautyrest mattress and the jogging pace of a beached sea lion. Lay a patch of rubber. The track is a great place to start. I recommend 440s, 880s and mile repeats. And no excuses. Let's shelve the self-pity and get out there. During our millions of years of evolution, nature has built in an adrenaline gland that allows men like you to outfox the public, outrun Whitewater prosecutors and beat the draft. That same adrenaline gland can also compel you to push the envelope on the track.

Run Farther. Sorry, Bubba, but jogging one mile does not constitute a workout. Not even Jack Kevorkian pulls the plug that quickly. The point is to keep moving. How? The answer can be found in that Faustian tale, Damn

Yankees: You gotta have heart. Miles and miles of heart. I recommend starting with 5 miles a day and working your way up to 10 or 15. Impossible? Unthinkable? Pshaw. Poppycock. Bushwa. In a world where Dan Quayle speaks and people applaud, *all* things are possible.

Run With Friends. Now that you're focused, it's essential to find a running partner to help you remain that way. We're looking for a reliable friend, not that vermouth-ravaged senator, Ted Kennedy, who's got about as much zip as road kill. Or Newt Gingrich, a man who moves at the imperceptible speed of a Rastafarian coffee shop clerk. I suggest that you run in the fast (and safe) company of the bow-wowsville Janet Reno, or the good-thinking, right-sleeping, ever-prospering William Bennett. I also recommend Kenneth Snoop Doggy Starr. Yes, I know, you have the terrible urge to take a shower in carbolic acid every time you get within five feet of the man, but he's got courage and endurance. And he's not afraid to tackle anything.

Just Say No...To Golf. Golf isn't a sport, it's a snooze fest. Tooling around manicured lawns in a golf cart while wearing triple-pleated polyester trousers, a pink shirt and white loafers is a travesty of exercise. The calories burned by playing 18 holes while listening to an asphyxiating torrent of golf talk can be replaced by consuming one vodka tonic at the clubhouse. You need to develop staying power, and you can't do that by practicing chip shots. Forget golf. Squeeze out sneaker juice. Your political opponents will be impressed by your energy. They'll think, "Don't mess with Bill. He's a runner."

Lose The Cigars. You're becoming a seroious cigar smoker, Bubba. The Washington control board has rated your personal pollution as "high." Yes, I know, cigar smoking is popular. Everyone (even Cybill Shepherd) is lighting up. But that doesn't mean it's a good thing to do. Riding a barrel over Niagara Falls was popular once, too. Besides, walking around with a cigar the size of a zebra's penis in your mouth looks ridiculous. Get rid of those things. Go cold turkey.

Give Up Fast Food. Look at you, you're the size of a tank. You've got to stop gorging on cheese pizza, butter-drowned baked potatoes and fist-thick, grease-soaked, bacon-wrapped, double-cheeseburgers with mayo and a large side of fries. A few more pounds and you won't be able to cross a state line without a trucking license. It isn't helping your running, either. Fast food makes you move as briskly as a Siberian road crew after a doughnut break.

I recommend a new strategic food plan: For breakfast, a bowl of Wheaties moistened in milk skimmed so thin you can read a newspaper through it. For lunch, a nice cholestrol-free bran muffin and grapefruit juice. For dinner, a large plateful of summer greens. Go on, toss in an unbuttered slice of bread. And let the good times roll!

Avoid Fast Women. First Kathleen Willey, then Gennifer Flowers, Paula Jones *and* Monica Lewinsky. You're a bad, bad boy, Bubba. Who are your advisors? Bob Packwood, Frank Gifford and Marv Albert? You've been spending way too much time around those moderately attractive, big-haired interns who follow you around the Oval Office as if they were puppies and you had a pork chop tied to your ankle. Word is, if the First Lady catches you cutting one more hottie out of the herd, you're history. She'll leave your marriage looking like Main Street Nagasaki after game day.

If reckless sex is your problem, I've got the cure: running. A good daily workout will make you forget all about women in low-cut, tight-fitting dresses. It will leave you feeling calm, peaceful and satisfied. You'll achieve a peace that no amount of food/liquor/cigars/sex can approximate.

What more could a president want?

ALL IN THE FAMILY

The runner and his family

I'm Going Now...Don't Try To Stop Me

A British mathematics professor recently announced that he has solved Fermat's Last Theorem, the most famous and elusive mathematical puzzle of the last 300 years. That's great. Now maybe he can turn his attention to solving one of the deepest and most complex puzzles in the world of sports—why does my wife get cold feet whenever it's time to go running?

We have two young children, so Linda and I run in shifts. She goes first, I go second. That's the way we do it. The problem is, while I approach my daily workout in a regimented, Boy Scout handbook manner—put shoes on, open door, go—my wife prefers a more casual I'll-get-around-to-it-sooner-or-later attitude. She does the dishes, reads the paper, watches the evening news...and then she goes running. Maybe.

My question is, why can't she get out there and just do it?

"I'm thinking about it," she tells me. "I need to change the water in the fish tank before I go. Don't worry, I'm thinking about it."

"Thinking about it?" I shout. "You've had four hours to think about it. How long does it take to get a thought started through your head so that it comes out the other end?"

"But if I don't get the fish tank cleaned now, I never will!" she counters.

Oh, she has her delay tactics. Believe me, she's got plenty of them. She can spend an hour lacing up her running shoes. Stretching can become an all-night affair. Her methods of stalling often border on the ridiculous, such as separating our garbage into piles, color-coding the Hefty bags and taping up big stacks of magazines.

"I'm going in a minute. I'm going in a minute. I'm going in a minute..." She's going all right, going through this chant like a robot with dying batteries.

Meanwhile, the clock is ticking. I could have run five miles by now. A dozen miles. A marathon. An ultra. I want to get out there. I'm ready to go. My desire to run is as wild and overpowering as the yen to scratch a chigger bite. By comparison, a sailor in port after six months at sea has a mere partiality to feminine companionship. Rush Limbaugh has half a mind to tell you what he thinks. And politicians are this-way-that-way about getting re-elected. Never has there been such temptation to run.

The really weird excuses are the ones she gets from the New Age health experts who say, "Don't do anything your body doesn't tell you to do." The idea is to exercise but not think about it while you're doing it. If it's work, then you're damaging your body's Mystical Aura, or something.

Evidently, you're supposed to surprise yourself with a workout. One minute you're just sitting in the Lay-Z Boy and suddenly you look down and say, "Oh my God, I'm running!"

When I find myself getting really desperate, I try to scare my wife out the door. I look out the window and say, "It's getting late. It's growing dark. If you don't get moving, you might fall in a chuckhole. You might get run over by a big truck."

It doesn't faze her. Nothing does. She's got such a case of runner's block I'm considering soaking her legs in Kaopectate. "I'm just going to fold the laundry," she says, "and then I'm going."

"Please, dear," I tell her. "Listen to me. I don't care if the laundry gets folded. I don't care if the plants get watered or the bookcase gets dusted. I just want you to get out there and run so that I can get my own workout in tonight. This week. This month."

"I'm going," she says, pulling out the Windex. "But look at those dirty windows."

"Look," I tell her, "we're not talking about an evening of blindfolded rock-climbing here. This isn't arctic wind-surfing or snake-taunting. It's just a run. Get moving."

Her eyes roll upward in a familiar arc. "All right," she says, heading for the door. "If you're going to be in such a hurry."

She's about to go! My heart flutters, my pulse quickens. Then—miracle!—she is out the door and running. But wait!

False alarm. She's back in less than a second. "Whoops," she says, sheepishly, "I forgot to feed the dog." By now I've reached my limit. It's time to let her know what I think. I try to pick my words to form a syntax less brutal, but there is no other way of phrasing it.

"You're never going to amount to much as a runner," I tell her. "Not the way you procrastinate."

"Oh yeah?" she says, pulling the vacuum cleaner out of the closet. "Just wait..."

My Logging Road and Lucky

I lace my shoes to the mocking chatter of the rain and slosh my way out to Lucky's kennel. She is already waiting for me, turning herself inside out with delight and ricocheting around the yard. How that dog knows we're going for a run is a puzzle. She can hear the rustle of clothing. She can feel the vibrations my shoes make as I walk across the floor. She can read my mind.

When I open the gate Lucky streaks from the yard. I don't need to point her in the right direction, she knows exactly where we're going on this cold, drizzly morning. We're headed for the logging road.

It begins as not so much a road, but a crack in the woods. A narrow path that pulls us up a steep hillside. The trail is gouged by rain and slick with clay. I am surrounded by the smell of damp forest and the close comforting feeling of tree trunks grown so thick your eyes can't penetrate a hundred feet.

Civilization falls away like so much sloughed skin.

At the crest of the hill there is an old, abandoned logging road. For Lucky and me, this is where the fun starts. The logging road is a perfect place to run. It is an eight-mile course filled with steep ridges, roller-coaster straightaways, sharp switchbacks, and the occasional leg-cramping hill that temporarily reduces me to a sucking blowfish. I give the throttle a quarter turn and stretch out my stride.

A mile down the road and we are soaked. The rain has weeped through the seams of my jacket and turned Lucky's sand-colored fur several shades darker. I don't mind. And neither does Lucky. My furry partner and I have run this road in all kinds of weather—everything from parched summer heat to freezing winter chill. We have run in fog as dense as anything heretofore seen in a Pink Floyd concert. My dog and I will take our logging road any way we can get it.

We head east, gliding past an imposing hedge of brush, dipping a shoulder and bending a knee to avoid low limbs. The road winds its way high and low through the woods. Here it clings acrobatically to a steep hillside, there it meanders through an aspen grove where a million vibrating leaves shatter the sunlight. Lucky and I move along like a couple of modern-day wolves.

This isn't a place to run sprints or time yourself. It's not flat enough or smooth enough for that. My logging road is primitive, watch-your-step, down-and-dirty running. It is also a private refuge and a reminder of some simpler era, a sort of crucifix thrust at the vampire of progress. There are no paved streets, no 7-Elevens, no angry motorists or trucks shrieking by with a suck of wind.

My logging road is a place where lost is a rule-of-thumb. The trees here are the trees there. Nothing in particular, all in general. Forest folds into forest, sky into sky. The solitude bends back on itself.

This is running, just the way I like it.

Lucky ranges out, but always stays within sight of me. Maybe because I'm the guy who doles out her Kibbles 'n' Bits. Or maybe her appreciation runs even deeper than that.

I once saved Lucky when she was attacked by a huge raw-boned, gangling Rottweiler. A dog that looked as if it had been put together with spare parts. The Rottweiler broke free from its chain, rushed Lucky and locked its jaws around her throat. Instinctively, I delivered a testicle-crunching kick that sent the big animal scurrying for home.

Lucky has been my close running companion ever since.

For the next couple of hours Lucky and I push up hills, challenge brush and sprint through owl hoots so raw with enigma that it would send half of America grabbing for the Valium bottle. Faster and faster we move along.

At the crest of one mountain the storm breaks and the sun pushes through the clouds. Far off I can see the town of Fieldbrook. Beyond that, all the ridges are shadow and light. A glance at my watch tells me it's time to head for home.

We hurtle back down the road through time. Before me, blurry with speed, covered with mud, Lucky runs smoothly, with a fine-tuned stride. As the road flattens and smooths back to civilization, I turn and take one last look at the mountains. Everywhere, for many miles, the wilderness is all one thing, like a great mirror, infinitely green and beautiful, always the same. This was what I had come for. I needed the solitude. I needed the repetition, and the dense hypnotic drone of the woods.

Lucky, on the other hand, just needed a good run.

Road Worrier

Hey! *Hey, buddy!* Watch where you're going. Oh sure, like you didn't see me, right? What are you, blind?

Sheesh. Guy missed me by inches...well, a few feet, anyway. Okay, if you want to get picky, a block. It doesn't matter, that was still too close. I don't like to take chances. Not when I'm pushing my daughter, Emily, in the baby jogger.

It's a dangerous world out here. You wouldn't believe how much there is to worry about.

Take the traffic, for instance. I didn't know there were so many crazy drivers...And pushy pedestrians...And steep hills...And mean dogs...And shoulderless roads. And I didn't know that I was supposed to bring something with me to put the dirty diapers in.

Before Emily came along I never thought much about that kind of stuff. Now I think about it constantly. Being a runner *and* a parent is no easy task. Sometimes it's downright nerve-wracking. I haven't gone a block and already I'm sweating like Pinocchio at the woodpecker's ball.

Excuse me...Yo! Mister! Look out, will ya?

For crying out loud, that guy cut right in front of us. Fifty yards closer and Emily would have been history. Probably daydreaming. Wake up, jerk! Smell the coffee. You should even have a cup.

Now let's see, where was I? Oh yeah, I was telling you about the dangers of pushing a baby jogger. It's *way* dangerous. Lumber trucks, chuckholes, campers, stray dogs, station wagons, pea gravel, tow trucks—you name it, it's out there. No wonder parents with baby joggers have so much gray hair.

I wasn't always such a road worrier, you know. I used to run to the beat of a different drummer. Say the drummer from Mötley Crüe. There was a time when I would zigzag through rush-hour traffic and think nothing of it. I would sprint through busy intersections with my Walkman at high volume. I would drink beer, run with unlaced shoes in the middle of the street. I've been on the receiving end of every mean look a motorist's face can shape.

That was prior to my enlightenment. That was before Emily came along. Since then I've moved into the slow lane and it's been a very positive experience. I enjoy running with my daughter. I wouldn't trade it for anything. We go out into the world, taste its many wonders, and come in contact with its richly varied populace. Sometimes we zip over to the mall so I can buy her a new dress or a pair of comfy Reeboks. That's always good for a little father-daughter bonding.

Time for a rest stop. Gotta change a diaper and check my partner's pulse. Her's is fine. Mine is through the upper atmosphere. Okay, looks like we're all set. Here we go through another intersection. Remember, Emily, don't cross until you see the whites of a motorist's eyes.

Whoa! Look at that. Look at *that!* Did you see that guy? He flew by at about Mach 1 speed. Probably calling a talk show on his car phone or faxing a memo to Congress protesting the 55 mph speed limit. Do that again, buddy, and I'll tailgate you to hell or any other destination of your choice.

Uh-oh, something has upset Emily. She's crying. I'll bet she wants to play with her toys. I'll reach into my bag here and, let's see, diapers, baby food, bottle, teething ring—ah, here is is. Her Fisher-Price wind-up radio that plays the best of Mother Goose. Oh, look. She shoved it in her mouth, chewed on a few bars, then thumped it smartly against my foot.

She probably prefers rap music.

I'll just get her bottle and put the business end into her mouth. There, she's stopped yelling and started chugging.

Anyway, as I was saying, I really enjoy running with a baby jogger. Emily likes it too. I get my workout in and she gets to see the sights. What more could a father and his daughter ask for?

Oh, sure, sometimes I get a little worried about the traffic, but don't misunderstand me. In no way am I laboring under the delusion that every car on the street will give us a wide berth.

But if they know what's good for them, they'd better.

Lycra Virgin

Over the years, I've introduced a number of people to the pleasures of running. So what that some of them didn't want to be introduced. They might otherwise have ended up as gang members, or drug addicts, or, worse yet, golfers. I'd like to think I've had some small part in saving them from such morbid fates.

One such person was my little sister, Stephanie.

Never in her whole life had Stephanie nourished a single fantasy about running. She considered it to be silly and foolish. The desire to run, she thought, had something to do with a deep-seated personality defect, or maybe a kink in whatever blood vessel leads to the adrenal glands. Or something as simple and basically perverse as whatever instinct it is that causes lemmings to rush into the sea. But then one day—and don't ask me how—the fog lifted! The clouds passed! Stephanie experienced a flash known as the "Aha! phenomenon," and the hidden world of running was revealed to her.

Telling the story, I am still staggered by the wonder of it.

It was a typical wet day. One of those soul-chilling, incessant, Pacific Northwest thunderstorms where the sky turns black and clouds boil up and sheets of water fall as in the Old Testament. The rain was steady. Endless. A perfect day for running. I found a race in *The Runner's Schedule,* snatched up my running gear and hopped in the car.

Madness you say? Sure, but it's a good madness. Ask any runner.

Since the race was about a three-hour drive from home, I decided to ask my sister if she wanted to come along. Perhaps in my last-minute desperation for companionship I skipped a few details and did not impress upon her the purpose of the trip.

"I thought we might take a little drive down the coast," I said, after honking my horn to bring her to the door. "You know, to relieve the boredom." And then I quickly added, "Oh, by the way, you might want to bring along a pair of shorts." She opened the door a fraction more and glanced up at the dark clouds.

"Shorts?" she said. "In this weather?" Thunder cracked stridently, artillery practice in the sky.

"It's just a little shower," I said, giving her my biggest PR smile. "It'll clear up. Trust me."

Inside my head armed ideas crouched. I thought to myself, if I can just get her to come along, maybe I can get her to run. At first, Stephanie refused. Then I told her that it was a bad day to stay home because the radon level was always higher on rainy days. Finally, she agreed to accompany me.

Minutes later we were in the car and gliding down the highway. The only sound was the whispery hiss of tires on wet pavement, the metronomic thump of windshield wipers, and Stephanie cross-examining me:

"Okay, what's this all about," she said.

"What do you mean?" I asked, innocently enough.

"I mean what are you up to? You're acting funny. Whenever you put on a show of being normal I know you're up to something."

Since we had already traveled 25 miles (too far for Stephanie to hoof it home) I decided it was time to level with her.

"All right," I admitted. "We're going to a race. And I want you to run in it."

I could tell Stephanie wasn't particularly enthusiastic about my plans, partly because she gave me a look that could sour non-dairy creamer, but mostly because of the way she sprang over and tried to strangle me.

When she finally let go of my throat, I gasped, "I'm telling you, sis, it's the opportunity of a lifetime." She glared at me.

"It's the opportunity to get soaked, you mean." The water on the road hissed like fingernails drawn across taut silk. Tick-swoosh, tick-swoosh went the wipers. She was beginning to weaken. It was just a matter of time.

"Come on," I said, "haven't you ever done anything on impulse?"

"Not anything crazy," she replied. "Show me a person who goes running in the rain and I'll show you a fanatic. Actually, I'll get the better of the deal, because for sheer spectacle a fanatic doesn't hold a candle to someone who runs in a downpour." I shook my head slowly, back and forth. Strange attitudes such as hers were to be expected of people who didn't establish a meaningful relationship with running early in life.

"It's not that bad," I said. "It's actually kinda fun."

"Fun?" she said. "What's so fun about running? For that matter, what's so fun about racing? And while we're on the subject, what's so fun about running or racing in a storm like this?" The questions lined up in front of me, just like that: three insistent bullies, hands on their hips and sneers on their faces, challenging me to meet them face-to-face.

What could I say? The penchant for apparent self-flagellation is confusing, at best, to most non-runners, and in some cases, utterly mystifying to the sedentary.

I wanted to tell Stephanie that running wasn't like any other sport. To be a runner you didn't have to be the best or even the fastest. I wanted to tell her that endurance, as opposed to raw speed, was within the common grasp, and that all you needed to be a runner was will and determination. And lots of heart.

But I didn't.

I wanted to let her know that competition is one of the most basic of human pursuits and that the thrill of victory is probably no less exciting to us than the thrill of the hunt was to our ancestors. I wanted to let her know that setting goals for competition adds an element of excitement to the effort expended on keeping fit, and that racing prevents fitness endeavors from becoming repetitious or boring.

But I couldn't.

I wanted to explain why I enjoy running: I like the way it leaves you feeling physically exhausted and mentally soaring, the way it gives you mental stamina to run when it's hot or raining or when you're tired, and the courage to know you can cope with other demands in your life.

But I wouldn't. Everything can of course be explained, but not necessarily understood. Some things have to be experienced to be fully appreciated.

"Look," she said, "I'll go to the race with you, but I'm not running. And that's that."

So, Stephanie was determined not to run, the storm was relentless, and the road was wet, slippery, narrow, winding and washed-out; in short, pretty treacherous. All in all, the day looked pretty bleak.

But things soon began to look up. As if by some heavenly miracle, just as we arrived at the race site, the clouds began to tatter and the sun came out.

There was a rainbow in the west. I glanced over and saw Stephanie trying to cover up a grin. I parked the car and went over to the registration desk to pick up my number. Stephanie tagged along behind. There was a good turnout for the race. All around us were runners laughing and joking. Others were stretching and warming up. And suddenly it happened: The Light was in Stephanie's eyes!

What's The Light, you ask? The Light is a sign of a sudden positive interest in running. The Light tells you that a person is almost ready to take the leap from non-runner to runner.

"Look around, sis," I said. "Check it out. No rock music blaring from the aerobics area, no multi-colored leotards and designer sweats. No attendant in a locker room, standing guard over his tin cup, holding towels for ransom. This is real athletics. Everything else is just rich boys' games." She listened in attentive detachment somewhere within her cloud.

"It does look like fun," she admitted.

I almost had her convinced. I approached the subject carefully, almost nonchalantly.

"They have a short race, you know." To this cue she rose like a trout taking a fly.

"How short?"

"Two miles." There was a moment of silence.

"Do you really think I can do it?" she asked, wrapping her eyes around her nose, as if facing the most agonizing decision of a lifetime.

"I know you can."

"Well, gee..."

"Come on," I said. "Don't do it for fame or fortune. Do it for the simple reason that it's there!" Her tongue poked through her smile and adhered for a moment to her upper lip.

"All right," she said. "Why the heck not?"

"A Latin scholar after my own heart," I said, bursting with enthusiasm. "Now let's get a number on you."

And so Stephanie entered her first race. As she stood at the starting line, I was as pleased with myself as if I'd just written a sonnet. It was incredible how well everything had turned out. In my wool gathering I hadn't noticed that the sky had suddenly became dark again. There are storms and then, I swear, there are storms. Just before the starters pistol went off, the rain started to fall with an intensity that beggars the imagination. Either that or we were caught in a tidal wave.

"A little nervous?" I said to Stephanie.

"Cold is more like it," she said.

"You won't be cold once you get moving." She shook her head and said something.

"Speak up," I said. "The wind is howling so loud I can't hear you."

"I've got an idea," Stephanie shouted.

"What?"

"Let's quit and go back to the car," she said.

"Quit? Never! You've made it to the starting line," I said. "The worst is behind you."

But it wasn't. The starter's pistol sounded and thunder c-r-r-acked and crashed. Lightning licked the sky close enough to bounce us off the ground. Rain came down in buckets. The race was cold, wet, miserable—enough to cause anyone to throw up their hands and think about leaving the sport for some saner pastime. Like cliff diving or amateur bomb disposal. I figured that Stephanie would never want to see another pair of running shoes again.

It's been said that for a first race, there is no course so fast and fine as a runner's memory. A first race not only lives on in the memory of a runner but thrives there, increasing in speed and endurance with each passing year. The worst storm in the world can't take that away. I was hoping all this would hold true for my little sister.

Then I saw her splashing toward the finish line, like a kid on the way home from kindergarten. She looked tired and wet, but she was beaming with pleasure. Purring with bliss, I gave her a congratulatory hug and slipped a jacket around her shoulders.

"How'd I do?" she asked, breathlessly.

"You did great," I said. "Better than great. You've just been through the worst race conditions any runner will ever experience. And you finished with a smile on your face."

"It was pretty wild out there, all right," she admitted. "There was rain, thunder, lightning and 50-mile-per-hour winds."

"Yeah," I said. "It was perfect, wasn't it?

When we got back to the car, I started the engine and turned on the heater. "Well, Stephanie," I said, handing her a cup of hot coffee, "is it something that you'd do again?" She sipped her coffee and mulled over the question for a moment.

"Yes, I would," she replied, wiping the water out of her eyes, "but only for fame and fortune. I've had enough of just-because-it's-there."

As we drove away I heard a sound. It grew in volume, swelling up and filling the space between raindrops. It was the sound of applause and cheering, the sound of a standing ovation for Stephanie. I think she heard it too.

Fancy Footwork

When my 13-year-old son asked me to go running with him last week, I was ecstatic. We haven't done much together for a while. Not since that little incident at the mall when, in a public display of affection, I made the awful mistake of hugging him—in front of his friends. Since then, he has been taking his phone calls in the closet, making totem-pole faces when I give him advice and behaving churlishly at the dinner table. If he can bring himself to sit there at all.

Adolescence is a mutinous, confusing time when everybody is trying to get off the boat. Since my son can't desert ship, he likes to criticize the captain. I have been informed that my laugh is too loud, my car too old and my personality too weird. That's why I leaped at the chance when he suggested we go for a run.

"I'll go running with you," he said, "but you gotta promise you won't embarrass me, okay?" The poor kid—he was really concerned.

"Don't worry," I told him.

"I am worried, Dad. I'm worried, worried, worried."

Good Lord, I thought. Worried three times. And we were only going for a run. What could happen?

Plenty, I found out. We hadn't even made it out the front door before I blew it. The problem, it seems, had something to do with my taste in running attire.

Just for the record, I've never been what you might call a stylish runner. But I do have my standards. I don't wear Bermuda shorts, knee-length socks or bargain basement running shoes. I may, occasionally, be guilty of wearing a Dick Tracy T-shirt, but that's it. None of this, however, was good enough. To my son, my running clothes were nothing less than a major source of embarrassment.

"Geez, dad," he said "You're not going outside dressed like that, are you?"

"What's wrong with the way I'm dressed?" I asked.

"Your running shorts. They're kind of, well...dorky."

I looked at my shorts. They were clean and unwrinkled. They seemed to be holding everything in place. I wasn't sure what more anyone could ask from a pair of running shorts.

"Can't you see?" he said, shaking his head back and forth, as he always does whenever I'm in the act of committing some gross social blunder. "They're way too new. There's not a single rip in them."

"No rips?"

"Right," he said. "And your shirt needs to be stretched out, too." According to my son, ripped and stretched workout clothes were in. Every teenager was wearing them. Perfectly good shorts ripped to shreds, and shirts that looked as though they'd been put on by climbing through the neck.

I didn't argue. Not with a kid who, in all important ways, was on the cutting edge of style. By getting out my pocket knife and slashing my clothes to ribbons, I managed to survive this crisis and prolong my son's life. I was fit to run in the Torn and Tattered Teenage 10K. But still the kid wasn't satisfied.

"Dad," he hissed, signaling me back inside. "Get in here, *quick!*"

"What is it?" I asked.

"Your shoes," he said, glancing around nervously. "You're wearing them all wrong." I looked at how I was wearing my shoes. I was wearing them the way I have always worn them—on my feet.

"How *should* I wear them?"

"You gotta unlace them," he said, "and pull those socks down. Hurry, before somebody sees you." Quickly I untied my shoes and pulled my socks down to my ankles.

"That's better," he said.

"What do I do with the laces?" I asked.

"Just let them drag. That's the way everyone wears them."

So, with clothes flapping and laces dangling untied, I stumbled off down the road. I felt kind of strange, but who knows? My son said I looked cool anyway. And of course, he was dressed exactly like me.

Good thing, too. If he'd been wearing anything else, I would have probably stayed home.

Sole Searching With Emily

There are moments that one treasures for all one's life, and such times are burned clearly and sharply on the material of total recall. For me, one such time was a Sunday morning one year ago when I put Emily Ann Martin, age 7 weeks, in the baby jogger and took her on her first run.

The route I picked was a little finger of a trail that crooks daintily around our town. The trail is bordered on one side by wildflowers and meadows and on the other by a clear, bubbling stream and a green breath of woods. Beautiful, yes, but the scenery probably did not convey much of an impression to my young daughter. Not that she was being snobbish, mind you, not at her time of life. It's just that to her the scenery was probably nothing more than a beautiful green blur. And since it had little to do with the large, overriding concerns of her life—sleep, milk and the condition of her diapers—the best she could do was to squint at the colors and move her small arms. That was all right though. I enjoyed the surroundings as we moved along, and I could try to communicate that enjoyment to my daughter.

A covey of quail clattered out of a nearby tree and flew off, transforming themselves from birds into scraps of brown confetti. "Did you see the birds?" I asked Emily softly, so as not to alarm her.

A little further on, a doe and her fawn pussyfooted across the trail just a few yards away. "Look at the deer," I said. "Isn't this a pretty place to run?" Then I stopped and kissed her cool cheek and adjusted her cap.

The scenery was actually a sort of gratuity on this first run for Emily, because what I'd brought her out to experience, mainly, was running itself. I figured that at this stage there existed no "dividing line" between my daughter and me, so that what I felt, she could feel too, through my communicating it to her.

Words alone, obviously, weren't going to do it, but I hoped that the sound of my footfalls and the way the ground moved beneath us would transmit something to her, some inkling of how important running was to me. I also hoped that someday, when she might experience these things for herself, some memory of those feelings might come back to her.

It seemed a good enough reason, at any rate, to strap her into the jogger, prop up her head with a blanket and take her (at an absurdly early age, according to her mother) out for her first run. It seemed, as well, a great excuse for me to go running while maintaining my disguise as a dutiful parent.

We moved along a slightly uphill stretch of trail where the early morning light leaned on the eastward facing mountains. I watched it slide the ridges southward, making a moiré on the varying leaf-faces of oak and madrone trees. At the top of the hill I stopped to rest and pointed to a swallowtail hawk, kiting back and forth across the trees. "Hawk," I said, very slowly and carefully, so Emily would remember it forever.

For every serious runner, there are thousands who run to hear the wind in the trees and feel the sun on their faces. Fun runners, recreation runners—call them what you wish. For them, running is not an ordeal, but a therapy, not an effort but a reward. When they run, they become completely absorbed in the moment, nothing else matters, and no other thoughts distract them from fully experiencing life at that instant.

That was the kind of runner I wanted my daughter to be. I wanted her to enjoy running, to seek out the beauty of nature in all its shapes and fabulous designs and to see the world through a dazzling prism of authentic imagination.

The miles innocently piled up on one another like so many gift catalogs from activewear merchants. When we reached the halfway point in our run, I stopped and picked Emily out of the jogger. She blinked at me like some very warm, drowsy bird. Then I sat her in the grass, gave her a bottle of milk and told her about some of the many advantages of running.

"You see, sweetheart, running is more than just a simple sport," I said. "Running allows you to live beyond yourself. It urges you toward excellence, it drives you toward quietness, it pulls you upward toward womanhood, but ever so softly, like an angel rearranging clouds."

Emily's head turned toward several bickering jays in the nearby brush. Undaunted by the noisy interruption, I went on. "Yes, running can do many positive things for you. But the best thing of all is that it allows you to direct your energy in a way that will bring a higher order to the world you live in."

The jays were squawking louder now. I don't think I had Emily's full attention. Anyway, it was time to go, so I put her back in the jogger and started down the trail. The next half-mile was flat and smooth, so I sped up and ran it at a delightful sprint.

I'm not a religious person, but after 10 years of running I must grudgingly admit a certain awe. A peek at enlightenment. Life flows and I am borne along in a river of sensations and smells; the faster I go, the more the wind squeezes tears from my eyes. I move, and I am deeply moved.

Another mile down the trail we were running alongside the water again. A fine mist was rising from the stream and a half-dozen ducks turned and swam away into the tules as if pulled on wires. Again, I'm not sure what Emily saw here. I hoped, though, that she could see how happy her father was.

I thought about what it would be like to have Emily run beside me when she was older. I thought about some day being able to run the same trail with her, and about all the great places that I could show her, running them again myself for the first time because I'd be seeing them through her eyes. Emily didn't have to be a runner if she didn't want, but I hoped she would be.

I wanted my daughter to experience the rich rewards of running, the world sweeping past us at just the right speed, the great, lusty breaths, the feel of wind on our faces, the glory of distance traveled. I wanted her to draw the vital connection between running and the spirit that, once experienced and understood, makes running not just a sport but a way of life. I wanted all the wonderful feelings running has given me to be part of Emily's experience of life as well.

Eventually, we reached the end of the trail and started toward home. I looked at my daughter, who was gumming a pacifier and contemplating whether it was time for her to start crying or not, and I said, "Thanks for coming along today. You were great company. I've got a feeling you're going to be quite a runner."

I think I may actually have succeeded in communicating something to Emily, because when I finished, she stopped gumming the pacifier, looked at me and smiled. I think I just might have gotten through to her.

No Known Cure

Something is wrong with my wife. She's been acting strange lately. I mean, really strange. I think she may be losing it. It started a month or so ago with her lingering perusal of an athletic supply store.

"I'm going to need some of those," Linda said, pointing to a rack filled with shorts and singlets. The clothing came in a variety of colors, most of it so loud it could have caused flash-burns on anyone who made the mistake of looking at it too long.

"Hmmmm," I murmured noncommittally.

By the time we made it out of the store, there were at least a dozen packages in my arms—and I hadn't put them there.

Next came the shoes. Footwear with a price tag that could make a grown man sit down to get control of his knees. Of course, last year's model wouldn't do. She insisted on state-of-the-art shoes—the ones with little computers built into them. Wonderful. Just what I needed. A wife with shoes smarter than she is.

"Hey, honey, how far did you go today?"

"Gosh, I don't know. Maybe I'd better ask my Reeboks."

Something else that wasn't the same; a not-so-subtle change in her eating habits. Meals, which previously consisted of items like pizza, cereal and cookies, suddenly became limited to alfalfa sprouts, milkweed soup, 20-grain bread and endless blissed brown rice.

After that, she stepped up her daily vitamin intake to the overdose level and started coming home from work later and later. Oh, sure, she came home happy. Tired, and sweaty, that's for sure. But happy.

I've been suspicious for quite a while, but now I'm sure of it: My wife is becoming a Serious Runner.

How did this happen, you ask? What caused this calamity? I'd like to say that it was the full moon, or the Ides of March. Or maybe because she broke her make-up mirror and received Revlon's version of seven years bad luck. But I can't tell a lie: I'm the guilty party. I introduced Linda to running.

Believe me, I had no idea she would become a mileage junkie.

Don't get me wrong, I like running. Who doesn't? Everyone wants to be a runner these days. And can you blame them? It's an exhilarating experience. Most runners I know are healthy—yes sir, they are! And happy—their grins prove it! Enthusiastic—why, these people never stop moving. They're lighthearted, intelligent and athletic—take my word for it. And they look good too.

But most runners know when to quit.

Not Linda. There's a quality of enthusiasm in her running that suggests madness. She runs before work, during lunch, after work, before dinner and after dessert. And when she isn't pounding the pavement in pursuit of high mileage, she's talking about it.

"Well, I ran today."

"That's nice."

"I ran yesterday—15 miles."

"Wonderful, dear."

"Tomorrow I'm going to run 20."

"Hmmmmmmm."

"I think I'll run 17 on Saturday and I might do 30 on Sunday."

And so on.

Pretty unsettling, eh? There should be clinics for this sort of thing, right? We have programs for people who can't resist a whiskey and water. Programs for cocaine addicts. Programs for compulsive eaters and chain smokers. We have programs for those who can't say no to a jelly-filled donut. Unfortunately, there is no cure for people like Linda. As all Muslims must go to Mecca, so too must my wife become a serious runner.

Oh, sure, Linda looks nice. She's never looked better. Bright-eyed with ERG and bottled water. Well-dressed and comely in her Lycra running clothes. Wonderful legs carved by the lathe of endless miles. Arteries that flow as clear as the spring runoff. A pulse so low she needs to look in the obits every morning to see if she's still alive.

But look at the toll it's taken!

Linda has worn out 48 pairs of shoes, seven running outfits, and—hold onto your Icy Hot—accumulated over 20,000 miles! Her appetite has increased; she carbo-loads like a UPS driver preparing for his Christmas deliveries. She runs through heat waves and cold snaps. She even runs in the pouring rain.

Why don't I do something? Are you serious? Ridding the planet of nuclear weapons would be a more realistic goal, you know? Not that I haven't tried, though. Even though I knew it wouldn't do any good, I asked Linda if she would cut her running time down to, say, a more sensible five or six hours a day.

She looked at me as if I had suggested she pan-fry the children for dinner.

Oh, well, maybe she'll eventually grow bored with running, right? Maybe she'll take up a second, more sensible sport such as full court basket weaving or hand-to-hand crochet. Right. A more realistic vision of the future might involve Linda walking around with a ski mask and a crowbar, looking for warehouse doors to jimmy.

Is there a lesson here? A word for the wise?

You bet.

You know the way cigarettes carry a warning on the package? Running shoes should carry the following: "SURGEON GENERAL'S WARNING: Certain runners will use these shoes for weeks in lieu of food, drink or sleep. If you see a friend or loved one becoming obsessed with running, hide these shoes."

There are psychiatrists who charge $100 per hour for that kind of advice. However, if you wake up at 4:00 a.m. to find your spouse doing wind sprints around the house, you might want to spring for one of those $100 sessions.

LONG MAY I RUN

The aging runner

Let Me Eat Cake!

The sky doesn't look as blue to me this week. The sun doesn't seem as bright. My training runs haven't been as enjoyable, and my running companions don't make me laugh. I don't even care about my next marathon.

I think I'm suffering from Post Junk-Food Blues.

I'll get over it. There probably are no long-term psychological effects from giving up 99% of the things I love to eat, like Twinkies and salami and pork chops and ice cream sundaes and...Ohhhhhh!

I had to go on a diet. My cholesterol was up, my mile splits were off, and when I yanked on my pants, it left me feeling like Andre the Giant had a death-grip around my abdomen. The decision to lose weight was a smart move. A logical move. A sensible move.

And I've been in a funk ever since my wife pried my fingers off that last pint of Ben and Jerry's ice cream.

It's the saddest thing on earth when you have to admit that you can't allow yourself a beer or a donut anymore. It's the end of your youth serving formal notice. It's the mother of all turning points. Big-time loss. Big-time transition. I mourn.

But facts are facts. I've arrived at the moment of adulthood when I need only look in the direction of delicious food for it to leap into my mouth and lodge in great lumps at strategic places under my skin. And it doesn't matter how long and hard I run. There it bulges buoyantly, while I sprint through another 10-mile workout, reminding me of the awful truth: I ate too much salty food for dinner and awoke this morning looking like the Stay-Puff Marshmallow Man, a parade float, the Goodyear blimp, flesh puffed up around my eyes like a Shar-Pei puppy's.

Once, when I was younger, this wasn't so. Back then, the chemistry of eating was hot and clean. My body metabolized everything I put into it. Cheese Doodles, butter beans and bacon, Hostess Ho-Ho's—I could pack it away.

And it was wholesome, charming, a signal of health and vigor; the world smiled warmly on me while I ate with abandon. Fried peach pie, double-thick chocolate shakes, hot dogs swimming in oil or sinking beneath a lava flow of cheese. I looked and felt terrific. It was safe, it was fun, it was friendly. Like savings bonds and milkmen and dogs named Rover.

I remember stuffing M&M's into my cheeks until they were grossly distended. A thousand cookies were dunked in coffee until they crumbled into the cup; I slurped up root beer floats, biscuits and gravy and hot fudge sundaes. Burritos and onion rings were definitive food groups. My eyes shone, my skin was smooth and clear, my weight never fluctuated an ounce.

Long days meant gigantic grease burgers, french fries and ghastly quantities of beer. I put it in my mouth first, and asked what it was later. Next morning I sprang forth shiny as a new penny. Fried pork rinds for breakfast? Hey, thanks man.

That was then. This is now.

Now I'm putting on a little weight. All right, the blobbo who shows up daily in my bathroom mirror has been looking mighty portly lately. The truth? Okay, I've gone beyond paunchy and obese seems within reach.

So my wife has turned me into a pea-pod puritan. She's been feeding me bunches of bananas, bushels of apples and those tasteless hockey-puck shaped rice cakes. She has me eating organic kidney beans and sipping carrot froth and spinach squeezings like an old rabbit with bad dentures. When we go out to dinner, she's got me building bean sprout mountains on my salad bar tray which make checkout clerks' eyebrows waggle.

And I'm sorry to admit that I've had to give up beer. I'm told by a friend that I recently had to be physically restrained from throwing myself in front of a moving beer truck. The emotion behind this Tolstoyian gesture was not, however, the suicidal despair of an Anna Karenina, but the intense desire for a brewski to moisten my parched throat.

Hey, I work out like an Olympian, why can't I drink like one?

What I wouldn't give for a 16 oz. steak shipped Federal Express from Wyoming, to which I could add several pounds of garlic and an equal amount of Tabasco sauce, salt and pepper. Served with a baked potato. Extra butter. Extra sour cream...Ohhhhhh!

It's gone forever. The sky doesn't look as blue. The sun doesn't seem so bright.

Throwing In The Towel

When I first began running ten years ago, I thought of growing old and slowing down as something that other people did. I was young and strong and running as fast as I ever had. Like a child, I truly believed things stay that way forever. I remember a friend and I were on a long training run, passing the miles and talking about upcoming races, when the subject of old age came up.

"What are you planning on doing when you can't run competitively enough to PR once in awhile?" my friend asked.

My blood curdled. Here was a wrinkle in the sport I hadn't considered. What do you do after you've climbed Everest without oxygen? After you've won the Nobel Prize? After you've added a couple of cogent points to the Theory of Relativity? There are, after all, some things in which one doesn't simply hitch up his britches and say brightly, "Well, then, on to the next challenge!" Running PRs is one of those things.

I decided that when the day came that I started slowing down, I would quit running altogether. I kept this thought in my mind for so long I began to believe it.

The years passed. One day I woke up to find that it had happened. I was growing old. All the signs were present: I had gray hair, a slight paunch and all the music recorded since 1980 sounded like somebody tipped over the china cabinet. Worst of all, it was becoming increasingly difficult to achieve the running fitness that I had in the past. Sure, I was training smarter, eating better and drinking less alcohol. But I was still slowing down. My running career was beginning to look more and more like the angst-ridden, emptily busy second reel of a foreign film. In short, I was history.

Despite all this, however, my thinking drastically changed. I decided not to quit running after all. Why the sudden change of heart? Whenever this question pops up, one person comes to mind: Lenny Escarda. Escarda was a long-time member of Six Rivers Running Club and one of the area's top runners. Lenny had many age-group records to his credit, including a 36-minute 10K and a 2:49 marathon. He was, in fact, the first person in the club to run a sub-three-hour marathon.

Escarda trained with an intensity that few could match. He ran 7 days a week for more than 15 years, logging 60 to 80 miles a week. Regardless of the temperature, Lenny was out there. He ran in hot weather, in rain, and on days when the wind-chill factor plummeted. The speed and determination which made him a top local runner spoke in every step of his workouts.

Then, Lenny's right knee started to give him trouble. It ached every time he went for a run. It ached badly. Months passed and the knee would not heal. Eventually, he went under the knife. That didn't keep him down. As soon as the doctor gave him the go-ahead, Lenny was back running. But before his right knee had a chance to mend, his left knee went out. The final diagnosis; major cartilage damage to both knees. Lenny Escarda's running days were over.

The running club was stunned. Why Escarda? Why the one person who loved running more than any ten runners put together? Those who had already taken their best shot at athletic glory wished they could exchange their knees for his. They ran mile upon mile in Lenny's honor, hoping to somehow transform their distance into a healing salve for his damaged knees. But no amount of wishing or running would alter the sad fact that Escarda's knees would not allow him to run again.

A more emotional runner might have succumbed to depression, but not Lenny. With his usual phlegmatic disposition, he took the news in a cloud of Buddhist calm. The club watched as he fought his way from hospital bed, through intense therapy, and back to fitness using the parts of his body that remained functional.

After a third operation, and while still on crutches, Escarda hobbled to the gym for a workout. Although his knees were aching, his spirit was intact. One year later he was again running daily.

After watching Escarda fight so hard to regain his fitness and adapt to the limitations of his injury, I began to think about my own situation. I suddenly realized how foolish I had been to consider hanging up my shoes simply because my times were slowing down. Lenny helped me understand that the real value of running lies not in winning, but in participation. Just as in life, the most important thing is not to have conquered, but to have fought. With this sobering realization, my philosophy on running has changed.

My body is growing old; that's a fact. I'm getting slower, and I've probably seen the best times I ever will. But Lenny has inspired me to adapt to those changes and fight the downward spiral. Maybe I'll have to give up a few vices. Maybe I'll have to cut back on my speedwork and take a couple of days off after my long workouts. Whatever it takes to keep running, I'm going to do it.

And I'll be thinking about Lenny Escarda every step of the way.

The Edge Of Might

Clearly, it's time to arrive at some sort of mandated retirement age for runners—especially for those about to turn 40.

The way I envision it, any runner 40 or older should be required by law to turn in their running shoes. I'm not saying you throw a shawl over their shoulders and point them toward the nearest rocking chair. But you make it clear that running is O-U-T!

I bring this up because my 40th birthday is just around the corner, and I'm experiencing the kind of fear and dread that only a philosopher like Kierkegaard could fully appreciate. I lie awake in the middle of the night listening for an irregular heartbeat and asking myself questions like, "When was my last check-up?" and "Have I been getting enough fiber?"

Other runners I know are more optimistic about turning 40. For them, it will be a delirious exhilaration of independence, a rebirth backward in time and into primeval liberty, into freedom in the most simple, literal, primitive meaning of the word. They can't wait for masters competition, for new PRs. They say, "Don't think of 40 as old. Let your personal crisis lead to constructive growth by becoming a more intelligent, creative masters runner."

I wish I could be so positive. Especially since (according to the studies I've been reading), my speed, endurance and VO2max are all about to take a long, slow escalator ride to the has-been basement. I've already started to experience depression ("I'm getting too old to be a runner."), physical breakdown ("I think my Achilles is acting up."), professional self-doubt ("Look for me at the back of the pack."), and the loss of youthful idealism ("I'll never get that marathon world record now.").

My optimistic friends assure me that age is only a state of mind. "If you keep telling yourself that you're over-the-hill," they say, "before long that's how you start to feel. On the other hand, if you work at staying youthful—if you think young—that's what you'll be. It's a self-fulfilling prophecy. Look at Frank Shorter, Bill Rodgers and Priscilla Welch. They turned 40 and were as competitive as ever—maybe more so. You can bet they don't consider themselves old."

I don't know, maybe my friends have a point. I may be losing a little speed and my body has become a little stingy with regards to certain juices that have all sorts of beneficial effects (only unpleasant things like anger or the proximity of death seem to open the floodgates). But at an age when most men are worrying about bulging waistlines and lamenting over scarcely remembered football games, I eat anything I like and smile at the knowledge that I'm physically as strong as I've ever been.

I guess things aren't all that bad.

Actually, running has a lot going for it; it keeps me fit and healthy, adds focus to my life, forces me to set goals and helps me develop mental stamina. Besides that, it's fun.

Quit running? No way. Mandated retirement age? Forget it.

I'm kind of looking forward to masters competition. Who knows, I might even set a few PRs. Maybe I'll give Bill Rodgers and Frank Shorter a run for their money. Nothing is impossible, right?

EPILOGUE

Final thoughts of an addicted runner

Running For The Fun Of It

I have been asked on numerous occasions (often by my wife) how I can write so much about something as simple as running. My usual reply is, "Running isn't simple." If anything, it's downright complex. One of the things I love most about the sport is that despite the most scientific training programs and mounds of professional advice, the learning curve is filled with unpredictable grades and unexplored terrain.

You can never know all there is to know about running (or yourself, for that matter). Each race is a lesson in courage and camaraderie. Each workout, a study in resilience and simple toughness. After 20 years as a runner I'm still discovering new things, still weaving a fresh understanding out of every step. That is, of course, what running does. It takes the miles and interlaces them to make wisdom, just as nature braids carbon and hydrogen to form the magic of life.

This book was woven together in much the same way. A story here, a story there, all of them plaited together to produce a virtual bumper crop of good times and hard-won wisdom.

For example, a run with my daughter (Sole Searching with Emily) taught me to enjoy the beauty of nature; A workout in the rain (Dressed to Chill) helped me understand the claws-and-teeth dedication that goes into training in all kinds of weather; My procrastinating wife (I'm Going Now....) proved to me that the toughest part of any run is just getting out the door; A DNF at the Napa Valley Marathon (It's OK To DNF...) allowed me to view running from an entirely different perspective; and an inspirational fellow runner (Throwing In The Towel) showed me that running, like love, becomes better with age.

How I can write so much about running? Because it is unique among other sports. Amid the lockouts, walkouts, drug scandals, trash-talking players, and figure skaters whacking one another on the knee, running sticks out like Charlton Heston at a Marilyn Manson concert.

Runners are some of the most laid back folks I've ever met, from the guy with the mongrel ensemble of dorky T-shirts, ripped shorts and dog-chewed shoes to the jaded SUV driving, junk bond trading, cell-phone-talking yuppie. They are like-minded individuals who use the sport to enhance life, to pump up the Zeitgeist. Running is, and always will be, the literal and figurative ground zero of fun and sportsmanship.

How can I write so much about running? Because for many of us this is as close as we get to religion. I have found the most precious moments in life jogging along a country road or striding down a busy street, listening to the smooth rolling hiss of my shoes, a sound of such sweet clarity that it drowns out everything around me. Small wonder that that each run beckons like a "Eat at Joe's" sign in a lonely desert night.

Races are equally enjoyable. At running events we are not treated like cattle, or rental cars at a NASCAR convention. All of us, from the first finisher to the last, are applauded for our participation. We are made to feel welcomed. Every race I've taken part in has been a kind of small scale cleansing, part head relief, part body bliss, part soul-satisfier.

How can I write so much about running? Because it has bestowed many gifts upon me, like the gift of freedom and childlike innocence. Remember running as a kid, when a jog down the street was filled with kaleidoscopic wonder? When a dash across town was gigantic and mesmerizing? When a simple run with your friends was a string of intimacies, a sum of small knowings, and one heck of a good time? Children run because it's fun. As adults, we need to keep that spark of fun alive, too. We need to let the child come out.

I've never free-climbed Half Dome or threaded the tube of a wave at Waikiki. I can't base jump off Angle Falls or ride fakie. But when I run, I feel the same sense of fun and excitement.

If one could bottle happiness, it might well be called running.

About The Author

Tim Martin lives in the Pacific Northwest town of McKinleyville with his wife and two children. He has written for Running Times, Marathon & Beyond, and City Sports Magazine. In 1995, he was selected as Road Runners Club of America National Club Writer of the Year.

About The Artist

Duane Flatmo lives in Eureka, California where his whimsical cubist characters can be found on murals, posters, and beer labels. For the last eighteen years he has found time to bring to life one of his Rube Goldberg-type human-powered contraptions for the Annual World's Championship Great Arcata to Fernadale Cross-Country Kinetic Sculpture Race. You may have seen Duane, a few years back, playing Flamenco guitar with an electric egg mixer on David Letterman's stupid human tricks.

more books by Marathon Publishers...

THE ULTIMATE RUNNER'S JOURNAL

- Double the writing room of similar Logs
- Cutting-edge advice from the sport's leading minds
- Full-color
- photographs Inspirational quotations
- Charts, tables, and a
- unique training map 192 pages, 9"x 7" $12.95

This journal will inspire the most motivationally challenged of runners.

Available at your local bookstore and better running stores.

For fastest service, fax your order with your Visa or MC number and expiration date to 916.492.8964 or:

Call Toll Free 1-888-586-9099

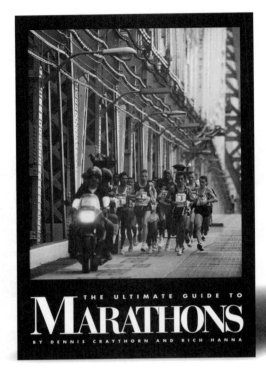

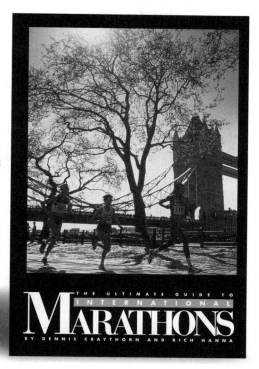